W9-CMC-981

# MICROJOYS

life

# MICROJOYS

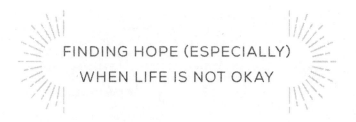

FINDING HOPE (ESPECIALLY)
WHEN LIFE IS NOT OKAY

## Cyndie Spiegel

PENGUIN LIFE

VIKING
An imprint of Penguin Random House LLC
penguinrandomhouse.com

Copyright © 2023 by Cyndie Spiegel
Penguin Random House supports copyright. Copyright fuels creativity,
encourages diverse voices, promotes free speech, and creates a vibrant
culture. Thank you for buying an authorized edition of this book and for
complying with copyright laws by not reproducing, scanning, or distributing
any part of it in any form without permission. You are supporting
writers and allowing Penguin Random House to continue to
publish books for every reader.

A Penguin Life Book

LIBRARY OF CONGRESS CATALOGING-IN-PUBLICATION DATA
Names: Spiegel, Cyndie, author.
Title: Microjoys : finding hope (especially) when life is not okay /
Cyndie Spiegel. Description: New York : Penguin Life, [2023] |
Identifiers: LCCN 2022033509 | ISBN 9780593492222 (hardcover) |
ISBN 9780593492239 (ebook)
Subjects: LCSH: Joy. | Hope. | Grief. | Attitude (Psychology)
Classification: LCC BF575.H27 S75125 2023 |
DDC 152.42—dc23/eng/20221017
LC record available at https://lccn.loc.gov/2022033509

Printed in the United States of America
1st Printing

Set in Adobe Caslon Pro
Designed by Cassandra Garruzzo Mueller

Some names and identifying characteristics have been changed
to protect the privacy of the individuals involved.

*To my mother,*
*Because of you, I am.*


*To my oldest nephew, RBS,*
*Because of you, I will.*


*To Ira,*
*Because of you, I can.*


*To my brothers and my nephews,*
*Because of you, I will never give up on*
*what is right, just, and possible.*

# CONTENTS

### PART I

## Observing Life:
## One Absurd, Ordinary, Miraculous
## Moment at a Time

* * *

PART II

Despite Everything,
We Are Still Here

. . .

PART III

Becoming Enough: Relationships
with Ourselves and Others

. . .

These are my stories and memories, and while I have tried to be as accurate as possible, I also acknowledge that these stories and memories may differ slightly from others'.

# PREFACE

*May this book serve as a reminder of the depth*
*of our human experience and the power of our*
*ability to feel genuine joy, despite it all.*

D eep in my bones, I know loss. Until writing this book, I hadn't considered how inter-connected the relationship is between sor-row, joy, and acceptance. In hindsight, much of my own experience of joy is built on a solid foundation of uncertainty, sadness, and grief. For many of us, joy and grief are steady dance partners in this lifetime and because of that, we learn to adjust to life *as it comes*.

As a biracial woman who is both Black and Jewish, suffering and grief exist profoundly in my own familial legacy. So, too, do resilience, joy, grace, and strength. Grief and loss have been close confidantes throughout my life. My maternal grandfather passed the year after I was born and my maternal grandmother passed before my seventh birthday. I have a few vivid memories of my grandparents, along with the memories gleaned from a lifetime of shared stories.

In the fourth grade, my classmate Laura was hit by a car as she excitedly crossed the street in her Halloween costume; I remember overhearing from adults that she was buried in that same costume.

As a child during the 1980s, I closely witnessed the AIDS epidemic as it ravaged our under-resourced community. Kids I'd grown up with were dying: Junior was nineteen; Edwin was twenty-three. Friends of my parents were taken, too, in the height of the epidemic.

I've only ever known impermanence. It taught me that though life may be fleeting and fragile, it is equally stunning and profound in its precariousness. What is here today may not be tomorrow; loss and grief are simply layers of a life—a life lived.

I also know the ache of belly laughter, the potential of positive thinking, the pleasure of good company, and the delight in choosing hope. And by virtue of all of this, I've come to deeply understand the necessity of microjoys.

## INTRODUCTION

Microjoys are a practice of discerning joy in any moment, accessible to everyone—*particularly* during difficult times. With time, this practice becomes a way of living because it offers us the perspective to observe timeless wisdom, understated beauty, and ordinary delights available to us in *every* moment. In spite of all else.

Unlike our culture of instant, relentless toxic positivity, microjoys require practice, awareness, and focus to take root. In fact, it was during the most difficult time in my own adult life that I discovered the revolutionary practice of observing microjoys. They helped me to restore my own relationship with hope—and joy—once again.

Within a four-month period, during a global pandemic, my thirty-two-year-old nephew was killed and my beloved mother passed away. One month later, my sibling had a stroke and experienced sudden heart failure. His doctor informed us that they weren't sure what state he would be left in because it took nearly twelve minutes to resuscitate him. My oldest brother and I— who had just buried our mother and his firstborn son— had to advocate tirelessly to make sure that our sibling was receiving the care he needed. He spent the next two months in the cardiac ICU. Because of COVID, we couldn't visit the hospital, so instead we relied on the telephone, calling three times a day for updates during this exhausting two-month period. (To this day, the sound of "on hold" Muzak played during phone calls still causes my heart to beat too quickly, leaving me expecting bad news.)* During this same time, with no explanation at all, I experienced an abrupt ending to a lifelong friendship—a friend I'd known for decades simply stopped communicating with me. And it all culminated in my own breast cancer diagnosis shortly thereafter. The diagnosis felt impossible to comprehend amidst everything else. But in that moment all I could do was acknowledge (to whatever God was listening) that I had zero control over any of it. And then, I fully surrendered.

All of this, dear friends, occurred within a ten-month span of time.

But here is what I also came to know during that same time frame:

*I am deeply appreciated and loved.* My community spans the entire world. And, from one pole to another, my community showed up with deep empathy and kindness when I needed it most. Even, or in spite of,

...............................................
* Our sibling is thriving and healing today. Thankfully.

not knowing what to ask for, I got exactly what I needed. The recognition of this beautiful truth is a microjoy that could easily have gone unnoticed while I dwelled deep inside of my own grief.

*The truest of friends sit alongside us through all of it.* And sometimes they show up under the guise of weird cat memes, rogue bouquets of flowers left on a doorstep, simply stated "I love you"s, and a whole lot of off-color jokes. Having friends who inherently understood me well enough to know that humor could temporarily break the spell of my grief: that, too, is a microjoy.

*I still have a whole lot to be deeply grateful for.* Losing so much so quickly was devastating. And. But. That doesn't change what I do have: a deeply loving husband, ridiculously funny siblings, a business built on forging connections, an inspiring and brightly colored home, hard-won honest friendships, vast community, and adorable (though highly disrespectful) cats. Appreciating that love and loss are close dance partners in this lifetime—that lesson is also a powerful microjoy.

Once we've journeyed the depth of loss—whether physical, emotional, tangible, or intangible—from the core of our being comes the capacity to seize every experience differently. To become more curious and empathetic, to live more fully and be less afraid. We already know what it means to fall to our knees in despair and pray to whoever is listening to *please, please make it all stop*. And in those times, we understand what a radical act it is to observe microjoys; to boldly choose moments of reprieve and joy even in the midst of heartbreak. One foot in front of the other as we slowly trudge forward. Or perhaps even as we stand in this moment, perfectly still.

Microjoys often emerge from the muck, similar to how a lotus flower resurrects itself out of mud over and over again. The beauty of this flower is that its roots are bound in the mud that it needs in order to bloom. Its perpetually beautiful reemergence is born of muck. Literally.

And in many ways, so is ours.

Microjoys transform the narrative of what it means to experience joy—from something ethereal and often unattainable on many days to a phenomenon that is genuine and deeply accessible for *everyone, always.*

In a world fueled by the constant buzz of outsized affirmations and a "more is more" mentality of happiness, microjoys are the polar opposite. Rather than loudly proclaiming who we are and what we want in an effort to seek out happiness, microjoys simply ask us to notice what is squarely in front of us. To acknowledge and appreciate the mundane beauty of what is already here, in the present.

Microjoys teach us to hone our ability to live within the gray, neither perfect nor imperfect, and still find beauty there, regardless of what may be happening outside of ourselves and outside of our immediate control. We perceive so much of the world in extremes, and often opposites. Good or bad. Rich or poor. Right or wrong. Happiness or sadness. Either or. But rarely do we perceive things as both. All of it. This *and* that.

Nonetheless, that exact place of this- and that-ness is where microjoys reside. Inside the wide gray area, somewhere between the vastness of black and white. The place of accepting and holding both *this . . . and that* as truth. Like deep grief and intermittent moments of pure joy, simultaneously. Those occasional moments of lightness amidst darkness are profound gifts that allow us the time that we need to come back to ourselves. And those gifts are the deepest expression of microjoys.

In life, we will experience moments of sublime happiness and, alternatively, moments of fall-to-our-knees heartbreak. All of it is essential to the human experience. And even during the most challenging of times, microjoys are still available to us.

Microjoys are revolutionary. They shift our outdated beliefs about what it means to feel joy by offering us the insight to reconsider what joy means, particularly during the most difficult times. Though it is sometimes necessary to lean into sadness, grieving, and anger when experiencing hard things, even then, we deserve moments of reprieve. When we are grounded in the darkness, we are still entitled to a sliver of light. And for our own resilience, hope, and well-being, we must learn how to let light in. Day by day and moment by moment.

Microjoys don't guarantee our happiness. Instead, they offer us the opportunity to consciously bear witness to joy in all forms, over and over again. They are momentary choices that shift our mind-set, long term. Experiencing microjoys isn't always the obvious choice (or the necessary one) but when we fundamentally understand that joy is often a choice, our perspective on life can transform into one of hope and possibility. Even, or especially, during our most difficult days.

After living through some of the hardest things, I could no longer sustain the all-encompassing, overeager approach to happiness that is deeply rooted in our culture. Only two years prior, I'd written a bestselling book called *A Year of Positive Thinking*. Though the words in that book still ring true, I've also learned a more equitable and sustainable perspective on joy that focuses on the subtle, often quiet moments that buoy and carry us forward. One experience at a time.

During our lifetime we will encounter the full spectrum of experiences: the beautiful, the not-so-beautiful, and sometimes the tragic, too. There will be moments that unmoor us from ourselves, but alternatively, moments that propel us higher than we ever knew possible with gratitude and happiness. All of it impacts who we become and how we move through the world around us.

Though this book is about the radical nature of discerning microjoys, my hope is that these stories also serve as a reminder that being present for *all* of life's moments offers us the opportunity to alchemize our experiences—the good, the mediocre, and the tragic—into a life that is still profound, beautiful, and deeply worthwhile.

Microjoys are not about picture-perfect circumstances. Instead, they remind us how wild, imperfect, and precious life is by teaching us deep wisdom and profound beauty within the awareness of every moment. Our responsibility is to be conscious enough to notice them. And that, friends, is what I hope this book offers you: a reminder to be conscious enough to recognize your own microjoys. *Because of* and *in spite of* . . . everything.

# WHAT YOU MUST ALSO
# KNOW ABOUT MICROJOYS

**W**hy *are they called microjoys?* Microjoys aren't small. Instead, they are easily accessible, and they don't require that we reach too far from where we are (in any moment) to discern them. They're called microjoys because seeking any semblance of great joy in the midst of sorrow simply wasn't accessible to me when going through the most difficult things.

During this time, the bare minimum that I could manage was to identify momentary insights and beauty in daily occurrences as I noticed them. But I could not reach for anything larger or further than that. Regardless of what life may toss our way, in the midst of busyness, microjoys grant us permission to seek out tiny, beautiful things without guilt or having to stretch to access them. We all deserve such grace.

**You don't have to experience death, or any great loss, to pursue microjoys.** They, unto themselves, will give you the ability to appreciate what *is* and the perspective to witness goodness, even in the unkindest of days. (Because those, too, will happen).

**Microjoys are different than happiness.** Happiness, though appealing, is a fleeting outward expression of what we feel, while microjoys are internal. They are immediately attainable, intentional, and deliberate— transcending temporary circumstances to buoy us. With practice, microjoys become a way of living, an alternative to toxic positivity and the cynicism of the everyday. They teach us that all things are fleeting but we can still be grounded in what is possible, joyful, and true.

*Microjoys are for everyone,* regardless of your culture, the color of your skin, socioeconomics, faith, sexuality, or gender. They exist for you as you are, right now.

*I did not create microjoys.* This is simply the name I chose to identify what is already our birthright. Microjoys are present so that you may find the capacity to walk through each day with more wisdom, deep acceptance, and a semblance of happiness, too.

Microjoys exist because you, regardless of your current circumstance, deserve to touch joy often. Even in the moments when you lack the perspective to reach very far to access it.

*They are always accessible.* They exist *despite* the calm or the chaos that surrounds us. And our *consistent* recognition of their daily existence offers us both the distraction and the focus that we need to find momentary respite in most situations.

*The more you acknowledge microjoys, the more prevalent they become.* The more we consciously observe microjoys around us, the more quickly our brains begin to easily notice them. For instance, consider the joy of finding your favorite "lost" pen or the satisfaction of a fresh glass of water first thing in the morning. Or the happiness you feel when you run into a friend in a seemingly random place. Or the surprise of encountering a rainbow from the prism that hangs in your window. All of these are ordinary yet fleeting moments. Or are they?

Without the presence of mind to recognize them, these magical, everyday happenings can easily be perceived as ordinary, mundane, and irrelevant. The divine beauty in these subtle moments can flee from our memory as quickly as they arrived. What a missed opportunity that would be.

But when we acknowledge what we observe and how we feel in these moments, they transform into incredible blessings that bring us joy that is firmly rooted in the present. The beauty is in their simplicity because they are the perceived mundane gifts of our daily existence, waiting to be recognized and seized. Right now.

* * * xxx * * *

And learning how to embrace microjoys affords us the rare opportunity to get to know ourselves—and our *own* version of joy—more deeply. Consciously identifying and discerning microjoys is a sustainable, revolutionary act of deep wisdom and self-kindness.

Through personal narrative and self-inquiry, my hope is that this book inspires you to see the world through a wider, deeper lens. Perhaps one that offers you insights into finding a semblance of hope in the most difficult of times, and also the most ordinary. You may find that some of the essays are contradictory. That is purposeful. In life we must learn to hold varying and sometimes conflicting truths at different moments. Many of these essays were written in real time, as my own microjoys brought me clarity, wisdom, and honesty. From day to day and month to month, that wisdom and clarity shifted to uncover the nuance and dimension of microjoys, often bringing with them paradoxical lessons. I hope that this book gives you the ability to recognize that you deserve to access joy and hope at any time, at any moment. That you, exactly as you are, can tap into whatever joy is readily available from wherever you may find yourself.

This book is not a compendium of redemption stories but is instead varying stories of life as it is. Sometimes that is redemptive and sometimes it is not.

But still and always, in the depth of all of it, there are many, many microjoys.

# PART I

# Observing Life:
# One Absurd, Ordinary, Miraculous Moment at a Time

The foundation of microjoys is subtlety. In an age of pro-vocative headlines and FOMO, we are deeply attuned to what is loudest and most visible, leaving little space for nuance, quiet beauty, and the absurdity of the day-to-day. So much of life occurs during the in-between. And while we are gifting our full attention to the shiniest objects, we allow moments of profound joy, humor, and meaning to simply pass us by. Like the rare sound of a bird chirping outside of your loud city window, the gorgeous light formation reflecting on the floor from a slightly open door, mistakenly wearing your underwear inside out (*Oh, that was just me then!?*), or the first time you notice you have the same hands as a cherished loved one. Ordinary moments like this happen quickly and within seconds they become missed opportunities for joy.

Microjoys require us to pay attention to the details and acknowledge the fleeting, often miraculous nature of the everyday. As you read these next essays, I invite you to examine your own ordinary and delightful moments of microjoy—those that you've already experienced as well as those to come. As you do, try to remember that it is a choice to "put yourself in the way of beauty."* And also in the way of humor and symbolism, too.

........................................

* "There's a sunrise and sunset every day. You can choose to be there for it. You can put yourself in the way of beauty."—Cheryl Strayed in *Wild*, quoting her beloved mother

# THE SPICE SHOP

My favorite Mediterranean spice shop is in my old neighborhood in Brooklyn. It's been around for well over a century. Though we recently moved, I return to the shop as often as I can. And every single time, I leave with paper bags overfilled with more lovely items than I could ever possibly need.

I walk in and am enveloped by the delicious smell of fresh spices, a multitude of olives, and more grains than I ever imagined could exist; bins full to the brim with goodness. I see the same smiling faces of the people who've worked there for decades. There is also the one man who insists on singing every time he sees me; it's equal parts embarrassing and charming, but that kind of familial recognition is just another reason why I keep coming back.

I take a number to purchase bulk foods and wander the store while patiently and impatiently waiting for my number to be called. I hear the sound of fresh peanut butter being ground, a cheesemonger talking about his cheeses in striking detail, and the hum of voices and languages that surround all of the daily activity of filling bins, buckets, and shelves.

On a recent visit I picked up (in no particular order) lemon salt, rose-petal preserves, Sicilian lemon extract, three kinds of olives, pink peppercorns, flake salt, and, of course, dark-chocolate-covered ginger. I'm still trying to figure out what to do with most of these items. But every time I see that jar of rose-petal preserves on my counter at home, I'm instantly transported back to that bright winter afternoon that I walked into one of my favorite little shops in Brooklyn.

A place that's been around this long could easily be overlooked as just a neighborhood grocery. But choosing to vividly see, touch, smell, and listen to what happens when I walk through those doors—that is the fundamental magic of being present.

### CONSIDER THIS

*Choose an ordinary place that you visit often and consciously decide to be present for every detail of your experience. Allow yourself to be fully there and experience* all *of it. What do you notice? What sounds surround you? What do you see that you may have missed before? What resonates for you?*

# THE POLKA-DOT GLASS

As if it knew that I'd need to be held and comforted during a time of great loss, my body became softer and more full. I was now two sizes larger than I'd ever been before. My clothes no longer fit; many of them, still brand new with tags, bought for the life I had in the Before Times. A metaphor for the way I felt after trudging through the last year: I *also* didn't fit into this new world in the same way that I'd once confidently sauntered through the old one.

My pants were too snug; my jeans no longer fully zipped up. I once attempted wearing a long shirt and just leaving my jeans unzipped (who would know, any-way?!). Eventually, I stopped the charade altogether. Instead, I wore soft cashmere pants, boldly colored caf-tans, and patterned floaty dresses. In hindsight, those pieces weren't very different from the ones I'd worn be-fore, except now, they weren't optional.

After months of feeling somewhat comfortable in my newly discovered soft clothing, it was time to let go of the tangible evidence of my former self. The one who *sauntered*, rather than *trudged*, through her life. The self whose body would never betray her. The self who knew, without question, who she was.

And so began an hours-long clothing purge of a dif-ferent life, a well-lived life. I thought I'd be sad and dis-oriented, but I wasn't. I pulled off my soft pants and tank top combo and purposefully began trying things on. Each too-small item was neatly folded and placed into a bag for donations. Three large bags overflowed with beautiful, once coveted articles of clothing. The bags swelled with my former life: from a crisp, brand-new, white designer button-down (to be worn with a bold, high-waisted skirt!) to an unworn, sparkly, hot-pink cocktail dress—the perfect dress intended for an invite that never came and a party that never happened.

After finishing up, I tearfully looked at the overflowing bags with both relief and delight. So many unnecessary clothes and so much weight unburdened. Lifted from my closet but also from my shoulders. I could breathe easier. I was no longer holding myself to a standard that didn't fit the woman I am today. And in this instance, fitting had nothing at all to do with size but everything to do with how I felt. When it occurred to me that I was transformed but still myself, I no longer needed to cling so tightly to the ghost of the woman I once was.

Two days and one carload later, I'd donated my clothing to a local mission thrift store. I was now figuratively forty pounds lighter and as free as a bird. But before heading back to my car, I quickly perused the glassware section. As if under a spotlight, there sat one brand-new polka-dot drinking glass. It was the perfect match to my decades-old set of polka-dot drinking glasses, the set with one missing glass that had broken the year before.

As fate would have it, my set is now complete. Again.

## CONSIDER THIS

*Look for signs. In a world that often shuffles us around haphazardly, I believe that signs are like arrows that exist to gently guide us. Rather than rigidly marching through life with eyes focused forward, allow time for meandering and contemplation. Take the detour. Peruse the glassware section. Do the thing you feel compelled to do, even when you can't quite make sense of why. In these moments, we come face-to-face with our own inner knowledge while also making space for the collective wisdom that exists outside of ourselves.*

# BIRTHDAY CAKE FOR ALL

**M**y mother was—is still, to me—the matriarch of our family. For as long as I can remember, she would bake homemade birthday cakes for each of her children. As a Jewish mother, she showed her enduring love through food. We all understood this simple truth: these cakes, regardless of how old we'd become, were not optional. She was going to bake us a cake, and we would graciously accept it.

As soon as my (now) husband became part of our lives, Mama started baking him a birthday cake, too. He had no idea what he was in for. Mom's birthday cakes were extravagant. Because of her generous use of fresh fruit, pudding, and excessive amounts of whipped cream, the cakes weighed a ton. Every time I thought she was done decorating, she'd add yet another garnish on top. With every dash of sprinkles and every spritz of cake spray, she was showing how much she loved us. By the time she was finished, we'd have a fifteen-pound cake with five different colors of sprinkles, three different fillings, and a full quart of whipped cream to top it all off.

Over the years, I attempted many conversations with Mom explaining the benefits of minimalist cake design. She wasn't having any of it. The kitchen was her happy place and within those walls, every decision was solely up to her. If she wanted more cherries, more pudding, and more multicolored sprinkles, then that is exactly what she would have. What *we* would have.

For all the times I tried to rein in her irrationally delicious cakes of plenty, today I'd give anything to have just one more sugary, overwhelming bite.

Mom had a willingness to listen, laugh, and bake anyway. She left behind a legacy of deep love, food for the soul, and a tradition of always recognizing one another with sarcasm, humor, and—of course—cake.

Over the years, I've eaten *hundreds* of her birthday cakes; enough to easily take for granted how much love she poured into each one. But with every bite, I recognized what a profound act of love and mothering was being generously gifted to each one of us.

**CONSIDER THIS**

*Is there a tradition among your friends, family, or loved ones that has become mundane and expected, that you take for granted? If you were unable to experience it again, how might you perceive it differently? Would you have more of an appreciation or show more gratitude? Would you spend more time being present while enjoying these traditions?*

*Might it interest you to write them down and memorialize them? Consider these suggestions to channel your own microjoys for (often) underappreciated traditions. Remember, these are all just food for thought.*

# IS THAT A GOOD COLOR?

An extraordinary thing happened while I was sitting in my local neighborhood cafe.

As the barista brought over my coffee, he asked a question that seemed so ordinary. So mundane. So unnecessary, even. But he asked anyway. A question that, to another person, might have seemed apropos of nothing.

"Is that a good color?"

I was instantly blown away by the insight of his seemingly innocent question. Here's the thing: I am serious about my coffee and I drink it with gusto . . . but also with half-and-half. And *that* was what he was referring to: the exact shade of my coffee when mixed with dairy.

As a devout coffee drinker, there are few things more perfect than a cup of coffee made with the exact amount of cream that will turn it a precise shade of caramel. It's a slightly brighter color than burnt sugar, and it's not beige, which is the color of coffee with milk. It's also not the dull gray-brown that I often see in coffee with alternative milks but instead, the perfect shade of coffee with half-and-half. The barista knew this about me and, in that moment, I felt so seen, understood, and appreciated in my peculiar reverence for the perfect cup of coffee.

Which brought back another *color of coffee* memory:

At 9:00 a.m. on a sunny Monday morning, I went to pick up my wedding dress from a tailor on the Lower East Side of Manhattan. This was two days before leaving for Minnesota, where our wedding would be held. I excitedly tried on the dress only to discover that it was a foot shorter than what it was supposed to be. My floor-length wedding gown was now officially a mid-calf-length cocktail dress. Yes, that happened. But here is what also happened.

After frantically calling and texting my closest friends to help formulate a plan B, I received the message that every one of us deserves in moments of distress:

"Don't worry, I've got you. Give me thirty minutes and I'll arrive with a cup of coffee in hand for you. And it will be the exact color that you like it. I promise. Everything will be fine. Better than fine, even." The. Exact. Color. That. You. Like. It.

In moments that matter, the comfort of knowing that you will receive exactly what you need in order to feel seen and heard—that kind of thoughtful comfort— means *everything*. It speaks to our human need to be understood. To be appreciated. To be loved. To be seen.

How wonderful that people exist in this world who understand how sublime yet fundamental the color of coffee is.

## CONSIDER THIS

*Our lives are filled with tiny moments, and within those tiny moments are hidden expressions of love and understanding. Choose not to ignore them. Choose to hear the messages behind the spoken words. Choose to feel the appreciation, understanding, and delight disguised by seemingly small gestures.*

# IN THE WOODS

While spending time away at a cabin in the woods, I awoke to a beautiful, almost impenetrable layer of fog one morning; a gray haze that settled over the deep red, bright orange, and lemon-yellow leaves of the trees. But even at the mercy of fog, the colors of nature could not be dimmed or made any less magnificent. The tree closest to me was filled with the brightest green leaves atop tall, twisted branches, all held safely by a sturdy but elegant tree trunk. A perfect tree for climbing.

And farther off toward the horizon, the tallest trees

were the deepest, most vivid colors of autumn, so alive and breathtaking. Brightly colored fallen leaves saturated the ground beneath them: a blanket of nearly neon yellow. How does nature do this every year without exhausting itself? There is so much beauty that it gives out so freely.

It was dawn and the lights that lit up the path around the property were still on. A nearby bench that I'd watched people congregate on all week was finally empty. If I didn't know any better, I'd say that it, too, was spending a restful moment taking in the wildness of nature.

As I stood in this beautiful silence, I was in complete awe at the wonder of the simplest things. Not only of nature, but of waking up, standing still, and simply being alive. How magical it all seemed.

I was overwhelmed by the idea that nature is simultaneously so powerful and yet so impermanent, too. Even a deep, dense, gray fog could not obscure the beauty of what simply is.

## CONSIDER THIS

*Though we can't walk through life fully alert every day, when you are able to, notice the details of what surrounds you. Acknowledge the colors, textures, sounds, and, perhaps most importantly, feelings in those moments. Allow yourself the opportunity to gaze—to really see the world in ways that you are not able to when you move too quickly through the day. Take time to be present wherever you physically are, whether that be an office, kitchen, beach, or even out in the woods. There is magic in the details (almost) everywhere.*

# THE UNSEEN WISDOM
# OF A BLANK CANVAS

Six months into the pandemic, my husband and I left New York City. We found an apartment with bright sunlight, saturated paint colors, lots of plants, and flowing open space, in a creative little town twenty miles outside of the city.

More accurately, we moved into a large apartment with potential. It housed a small, glassed-in sunroom (which eventually became my office), two bathrooms (unheard of in most New York City apartments), built-in bookshelves (so fancy!), and lots of crown molding (even fancier!).

While seeing it for the first time, my initial impression of the space was that it was tastefully decorated, dimly lit, and very beige overall. It wasn't quite *us*, and yet, it also felt like it could be our next home. My husband, who is a photographer, has an incredible eye for spaces, so before signing the lease, he requested that the entire apartment, crown molding and all, be painted bright white. I wasn't as committed to this idea as he was but I also knew that I would not be happy with the cream-colored walls that come standard with many rentals. (Note: Because I can already feel the seething from readers and friends with beige walls, please let me clarify: I love *your* cream, eggshell, and beige walls. Truly, I do! And just like cool, bright white walls aren't everyone's taste, the same is true of warm, neutral colors, too. It's not personal and my husband and I would love to still be invited to your home for dinner, drinks, movie nights, BBQs, etc. Thank you for understanding . . . and for your continued future invitations. Onward!)

I remember walking into the apartment for the first time after the space was painted; I was stunned by how much larger and brighter it looked. In that moment, it became the perfect blank canvas to become our next home. Having no idea that my world was about to collapse, we got down to work designing and decorating our new apartment. (This was two months after my nephew passed, and in another two months, my mother would join him.)

We created a statement wall in the center of the apartment with colorful, floral wallpaper and hung an oversized portrait on top of it. Across from our (working) fireplace, we painted the widest wall in our living room a bright marigold yellow. Another wall (in a different room) was painted a deep navy blue and yet another was painted a calming shade of coral.

We bought a beat-up old metal media cart (the kind that your fifth grade teacher would roll in with the projector for movie days) and had it powder-coated in a bright shade of hot pink. It lives in our dining room below one-of-a-kind works of art that hang on our walls. After Mom died, we inherited her vast plant collection; they thrive beautifully throughout our home, amidst all of the light, color, and open space.

When we moved away from our tiny-but-beloved Brooklyn apartment, we couldn't have envisioned what was in store for the year that followed. Though in hindsight, there is no more perfect place for healing than where we are today, in the comfort of our deeply unique-to-us, brightly colored home, with neighbors to share wine in the yard with and a community of creativity, joy, and calm after the storm.

**CONSIDER THIS**

*There is no perfect recipe that will heal what breaks within us. But there is the well-worn knowledge that, with time, things will be okay nonetheless (whatever okay means for you). It doesn't take away from what is true, it doesn't make loss more bearable, it doesn't immediately heal our brokenness. But with each decision made and tiny step taken, we find the wisdom buried underneath the tumult. And it may just help us to find our way out of the rubble and into the light, once again.*

# A GLASS PIGGY BANK

On a business trip out West, I picked up a crystal-clear glass piggy bank from a local shop. I had no particular reason for buying it and no specific person in mind to gift it to. I simply fell in love with it and allowed myself the indulgence of not needing any justification to purchase it.

When I arrived back home, I placed it on a shelf temporarily until I could figure out what to do with it. As the days turned into weeks, I'd drop coins—and sometimes bills—inside. There were two very lucky occasions that twenty-dollar bills made their way in as well.

After about a year, the little glass pig overflowed with money, and all of it was *found*. Shiny pennies discovered in puddles, a nickel left behind on a subway seat, a handful of change from the pocket of a thrifted jacket, a twenty-dollar bill left unclaimed on the floor of an empty elevator. Money, in all denominations, seemingly kept appearing wherever I went.

Of course, finding money is a microjoy, an ordinary lovely surprise. But another near-missed microjoy is the recognition that in not having a specific reason for buying this little glass pig, I'd inadvertently given us a clear vessel to tangibly witness the abundance found in simply paying closer attention to the world around us. And in recognizing that, we experienced so much more of it. Since then, we've purchased a second matching glass piggy bank. It, too, is almost full.

Long live small indulgences.

## CONSIDER THIS

*Without a practical reason to do so, buy, barter, or acquire something\* you're drawn to simply because it makes you happy. This isn't about spending money; instead, it's about allowing yourself to receive small gifts and recognize the longer-term impact of such gifts, whether that impact arrives in smiles, abundance, humor, or any other microjoys.*

......................................................

\* The size or item doesn't matter.

# FRECKLE FOOD FACE

I have a freckled face. I always have; I suppose I always will. I also have a tan three-inch birthmark on the left side of my face that has become nearly invisible with age. I was teased terribly about this birthmark as a child, when it appeared larger on my much smaller face. I was teased so badly that when I was ten years old, I asked my parents if I could have it removed, to which my mom said that if I still hated it when I was sixteen, we could do that. In hindsight, this was excellent though *highly* dishonest parenting because, though I felt like there was an end in sight to the constant mocking, we absolutely did not have the means for cosmetic surgery. Not surprisingly, my birthmark is still on my face. I am glad for this.

As an adult, I've always admired features that are more unique, like a space between two front teeth (diastema, it's called), a randomly placed beauty mark, naturally bright-orange hair (my mom was a redhead in her heyday), or facial features that are different than what is traditionally perceived as beautiful, which I find to be mostly just boring.

But back to freckles. Something weirdly magical happens with freckles. And unless you have them, the degree to which this transformation takes place is hard to visualize.

During the summer, my freckles (formerly in hiding) become bright and intense, taking over my chin, forehead, and nose in areas that were mostly freckle-free during the rest of the year. They transform from a subtle muted beige against tan skin to a startling, almost 3D brown when the sun comes out.

They change so dramatically that I recall looking in the mirror one morning and spying a new patch of freckles on the lower right corner of my face that, in my recollection, wasn't there previously.

Except upon closer inspection, they weren't freckles.

It was . . . wait for it . . . *lentil soup* that was still on my cheek from dinner the night before.*

## CONSIDER THIS

*Don't wash your face and perhaps you'll be lucky enough to find remnants of the previous night's meal the next day, too. Delightful! Or if you'd prefer to keep things simple, wash your face often and avoid this tragic scenario altogether.*

...........................................

* Hold your judgments about my dirty face; my dermatologist asked that I not wash my face daily because it's too drying for my particular skin type. So sometimes, when I haven't worn makeup, I don't wash my face at night. I am still a (mostly) good person. And I am still (mostly) ashamed of this incident.

# SITTING IDLE

This is an essay about complete and utter nothingness. Do not expect excitement or surprises. You've been warned.

While trying to write, I often sit around doing nothing except observing quietude and avoiding distraction. What started off as a boring exercise in its impracticality has instead created a spaciousness that is restorative in ways I can't easily explain.

I sit on our blush-colored sofa, wrapped in a double-thick fleece blanket, and spend minutes perusing our home from that vantage point; looking at the books on the shelves, half smiling at the framed pictures of loved ones, watching the sunlight dapple the plants, and observing Shaker, our younger cat, lying around in wait for nothing at all to happen. Because really, *nothing at all happens*. His eyes are wide with expectation and I blurt out (to no one, since I'm home alone aside from the cats): "You're in for a rude awakening, cat. Nothing is going to happen here so go back to sleep." I realize that I just spoke aloud *to a cat* and though I'm briefly embarrassed for myself, I continue my enthusiastic quest for nothingness.

To break up the monotony, I get up and make a cup of coffee. On my way to the kitchen, which is only a few feet away, I pass our full-length mirror and realize that I am wearing more layers than could possibly be necessary inside a well-heated apartment: shearling slippers, wool socks, velour soft pants, a tank top, and an off-the-shoulder knee-length sweater dress (and still, my fleece blanket awaits me on the sofa). My curly hair has been loosely clipped up so many times that half of it is no longer pinned up at all and the other half has four different hair clips visible. (There may be more but these are the ones I can see.) I look ridiculous and something about catching a glimpse of myself in full disarray in the middle of a workday makes me feel giddy and rebellious. Though it's times like this when I question whether I have adequate adult supervision when my husband, Ira, is away, these moments also instill me with an (oddly) empowered sense of self. In spite of everything, I've created a life that allows me to look absurd, talk to cats, and take coffee breaks whenever I want to. That has to mean something commendable, right?

I finally make it to the kitchen. When I'm done, hot cup of coffee in hand, I move to a different spot in the living room, this time sitting down in our corner chair, and again, I do nothing. Nearby are last week's newspaper and piles of various books. I contemplate picking one up but I know each is only partially read, so choosing a book would mean having to catch up to the part where the bookmark was left. I cannot use mental space for that right now so the books will have to sit awhile longer, untouched but inspiring from afar, nonetheless.

Sitting quietly allows me to write without judgment and have thoughts that don't require further exploration. Like feeling the wind graze my skin on a warm day, thoughts simply come and go with no attachment, but leave me a tiny bit better than before. What a rare blessing that is in a culture that begs for every moment of our attention to be purposeful and productive. Idleness, in all its boringness, is incredibly underrated.

**CONSIDER THIS**

*You may find that doing nothing is more difficult than you expect. In my own experience, it takes practice. The perception of wasting time feels counter to so many of our cultural beliefs. "Get busy living or get busy dying." "Idle hands are the devil's* workshop." There are countless sayings that caution us against boredom, idleness, and doing nothing. My response is still: DO. MORE. NOTHING. Numbing ourselves with constant distractions does not equate to a life well lived—but perhaps creating space for deep rest and moments of quiet could.

# SEEMA'S MASALA CHAI

I found myself adrift in New York City. I had just quit my job of eight years. I hadn't yet decided to leave the fashion industry altogether, but I knew that something had to change. Uncertain of what to do next, I called my favorite (very wise) graduate school professor and friend for advice. Outside of teaching, he researches the impact of globalization on the world. When I called, he picked up the phone from his home in Delhi. A month later, he'd be heading to Nepal, where he would stay for several months to study the regional nomadic people.

I spent a few minutes hurriedly explaining my uncertainty. As soon as I finished talking, he said plainly, "Come to India, I'll pick you up at the airport." Two weeks later, I boarded a sixteen-hour flight.

I spent the next few weeks exploring life, praying in temples, visiting the Taj Mahal, shopping for colorful objets d'art in Jaipur, and eating deliciously spiced foods.

In Delhi, my friend's longtime friend and cook, Seema, would wake me up at 6:00 a.m. each day with a cup of steaming hot chai. In the final days of my trip, I asked Seema if she'd awaken me when she arrived, which was usually around 5:00 a.m., so that I could learn how to prepare this magical gingery concoction. This started a new morning routine where she'd sit at the foot of my borrowed bed, directly in front of the space heater, and speak to me in Hindi for several minutes, slowly waking me up. I'd speak back to her in English. Though neither of us understood the words being exchanged, we clearly understood the gestures, smiles, and sentiment. I was later told by my friend that we both referred to one another as "sister" in our mother languages. She and I hugged for several moments before my departure back to the States.

Over a decade later, that first trip to India still fills a space deep inside my heart. As the weather gets cold on the East Coast each autumn, I continue to make Seema's delightful chai recipe, taking great care with each ingredient, allowing it to simmer for the full twenty to thirty minutes that it needs to blossom.

And because microjoys are that much more special when shared, below is that recipe as I learned it.

## Seema's 6:00 a.m. Masala Chai

*(Makes approximately 2 cups)*

Fresh ginger: 1½–2" or more to taste, diced

Cardamom pods: 8–10

Whole cloves: 8–10

Cinnamon bark (or sticks if bark isn't available): several pieces of bark or 3–4 sticks

Cardamom powder: ¼ teaspoon

CTC black Assam tea*: 1½ tablespoons

Demerara sugar: I buy sugar cubes and use about
4–6 cubes per pot. Add any amount, to your taste.

Whole milk: ¼ cup or more to taste

Almonds (optional)

**DIRECTIONS:**

Boil the ginger, cardamom pods, cloves, cinnamon
bark, and cardamom powder in about 3 to 4 cups of
water for 20 minutes. Then add the Assam tea leaves,
sugar, and milk and simmer for another 5 minutes or
so. Slowly strain the tea into a heat-resistant glass.
Add whole almonds to the hot tea and enjoy. (And
of course, eat the almonds when your tea is finished.)

......................................................

* I prefer CTC tea better than traditional loose-leaf for this recipe because
it tastes richer and is what is traditionally used in India. CTC means crush,
tear, curl.

**Note**: On my trips to India (this one and my honeymoon, years later), chai was often served in a thick glass rather than a mug. But be warned: the cup will be *very* hot. To me, this is simply part of the experience; it takes a lot longer to savor chai while simultaneously attempting to hold a piping hot cup in both hands. Sip. Put the glass down. Pick it up. Sip. Put the glass down. Repeat. Savor *each* sip.

### CONSIDER THIS

*Whenever possible, allow life to happen without a checklist or a plan. And when you do make space for this, savor the delight of experiences by being curious. Ask questions. Observe. Learn from others. And remember that words are not the only way that we communicate that which is in our soul.*

# THE WORLD AS IT WAS

It was the six-week mark in quarantine in our cozy (read: tiny) Brooklyn Heights apartment. We spent a lot of time learning about (*erhm*, and drinking) various wines. So much so that our local wine-shop owner would email me personally when our favorite biodynamic wines came back into stock. But in addition to becoming (much) more well informed about grapes, I'd also spent time creating a photo book of our first forty days in quarantine. I didn't want to forget the significance of this time.

I'd been primarily in New York City since 1999,

when I arrived for college. I moved to the city permanently a few years later.

In 2001, I witnessed the collapse of the Twin Towers from the seventeenth floor of my office building in midtown. It was my friend Marnie's first day at the same company where I worked; 9/11 was also her twenty-first birthday. Together, we watched the towers collapse. Somehow we found ourselves accepting two Xanax from a well-dressed, equally shocked stranger on Fifth Avenue. (We were fine but I do not recommend taking pills from strangers. Ever.) While covered in a coating of Twin Towers dust mixed with disbelief, we wandered aimlessly downtown until well into the late evening; there was no cellular service and neither of us could get home because the trains were out of service. I'd never seen my entire family gathered as tightly as they were when I finally made it back home to central New Jersey around 2:00 a.m. on September 12. We all cried.

I was also in New York for the August 2003 blackout that shut down the city. Four of my coworkers and I dined on one piece of chocolate and three slices of leftover cold pizza from my boss's fridge. That's all she had. We worked in fashion in the early 2000s. I'm certain that having so little food in the refrigerator wasn't abnormal. It was a hot NYC summer and there was no air conditioning so we all slept half naked in her one-bedroom apartment because we couldn't get to our respective homes. Actually, now that I'm thinking back: some of us wore her boyfriend's boxers to bed but I suppose that's a story for another day. Ah, being twentysomething in NYC.

Almost a decade (and much debauchery) later, in 2012, I was living alone in Brooklyn Heights when Hurricane Sandy tore through the city and flooded entire neighborhoods. My garden-level apartment was ultimately unaffected but just in case, a friend left me the keys to her fifth-floor apartment a few blocks away, where she had all the things needed for city survival, like bottled water, flashlights . . . and a doorman.

Somewhere between our two apartments, I ordered myself an old-fashioned from the bar of the restaurant that was, coincidentally, at the corner of the street my husband and I moved to together several years later.

I was also there in 2016 when we had the largest blizzard in NYC's history. There were no working subways and everything seemed to come to a standstill for weeks. I was on a bus across Brooklyn to attend a friend's yoga class when a large cockroach climbed up the carpeted wall next to me. (Yes, older city buses had half-carpeted walls for some inexplicable reason.) I was so emotionally wrung out that I didn't even care—I just scooted over and let him pass. Go forth, cockroach.

And here we were: New York City in 2020. The bittersweet truth was that I didn't think we would be in this fine city for whatever was to come next. I was no longer in my twenties or even thirties and I was married, with a very different life than the one I'd once lived.

The world that we lived in three months before no

longer existed, and it never would again. We couldn't go back to the way it was prepandemic. We were changed, and so was everyone around us. New York will always be one of the most resilient, exhilarating places in the world—and still, it won't ever again be the Before Times.

Knowing that our time in New York City was coming to a close, I didn't want to forget what we collectively were experiencing at that moment. It was both heartbreakingly sad and excruciatingly beautiful: the hand-drawn paper rainbows in windows that represented better times ahead, permanently closed storefronts, cocktail delivery (which was illegal any other time), using Clorox wipes to sanitize money, an impractically long daily skincare routine (my face is still baby soft because of this), talented musicians performing from their fire escapes, the weight I'd put on by sitting around for so long, loss of all kinds, the love of my husband, home-baked banana bread, frantic text messages, fighter jet salutes for essential workers, and reconnecting with my dearest friends. All of it. The hard stuff but also the most tender moments, too. I wanted to remember how it all felt; the rainbows particularly, the literal ones and the figurative.

This is why I chose to compile hundreds of random photos taken for forty days, beginning on March 16, 2020. That year changed me indelibly and I didn't want to forget the initial moments that transformed me into whoever I was to become.

**CONSIDER THIS**

*Life is filled with paradoxes, and darkness and light often end up converging.*

*With patience and bravery, we must stay awake and present for all of it: the seductive goodness and the hardships, too. Bear witness to what is, because each moment has the capacity to transform and propel us forward in ways that might otherwise* never occur unless we are present enough to notice them. Accepting paradox allows us to stay both soft and firm in life, which reminds me of a quote from Brené Brown in Braving the Wilderness: "Strong back, soft front and wild heart." There are moments in life when we must accept that *both* this *and* that *can be true.*

Write things down. Document all kinds of experiences often, whether through pictures, artwork, or shared conversation. The convergence of opposites is where we learn the perseverance to gently hold grief in one hand and joy in the other. And what a necessary lesson that is.

# MY EYES ARE STARVING

*It's a famine of beauty; it's a FAMINE OF BEAUTY,*
*honey. My eyes are starving for beauty!*

—André Leon Talley, larger-than-life fashion
editor, journalist, and "man of grand
pronouncements," in *The September Issue*

I love discovering the sublime in the simplicity of
life. Sunlight streaming through a window, elec-
tric cars that make no sound (How is this even
possible? Shhh, I don't really want to know), watching
my cat Jake's leg (which I thought until recently was an

arm) hang down the side of the sofa like he's reaching for something (except that he's actually asleep in that position), or the subtle way that a particular shade of red lipstick makes my skin look glowy during an otherwise unexciting video call.

There is so much magic around when we are clear enough to witness it.

Sharing a bottle of wine with the neighbors that we barely know on a warm summer evening. Answering the phone to hear your friend's voice in the age of texting everything. Seeing the bright pink flower outside my window that refuses to die, even during a winter cold snap. Having small talk about nothing of importance with the other people in line at Whole Foods. Watching our five-year-old niece exclaim that she is a genius for wrapping herself in her nana's poncho and putting her two favorite stuffed animals in the pockets while she creates a bedroll out of a yoga mat and a living room pillow. Seeing the snow weigh down the plants outside whose greenery is peeking through anyway as if to say "Not today, Satan" to the freshly fallen snow. Or passing a jogger on the street and giving each other the "I see you out here being healthy and looking fabulous" nod, regardless of how *not* fabulous we might feel in that moment.

Oh! Or the first bite of a warm, crispy loaf of French bread . . . eaten at a cafe in New Jersey. Or the bright shiny color of a fresh manicure. Also. That very big house that is painted in several shades of purple. How fun! Or the way my brother takes entirely too much time telling what should be a very short story. (This may or may not run in our family.)

How thick cashmere sweaters feel on my skin in winter. Or walking barefoot indoors on hardwood floors or feeling the warmth of a wool rug underneath my cold feet when I first step out of bed in the morning. And how Ira smiles: the corners of his eyes crinkle up and his dimples become so deep that I can't help but poke my finger in them. Or hearing the water flow from our cats' plastic water fountain and closing my eyes to pretend momentarily that life is always this serene.

And this is a big one: shopping at a grocery store and recognizing that I don't actually *have* to look at the prices of what I'm buying anymore (though I do because *why are things so expensive?*). Or feeling comfortable enough to sit alone and order a meal while chatting with strangers and people-watching instead of busying myself by looking at my phone. Ooooh, or going to a Tuesday matinee and ordering a large bag of buttery, salt-laden popcorn and feeling as though I'm cheating on my adult responsibilities by not working at that midday hour. And also! Owning various gorgeous dresses for no particular reason except in preparation for when I'll need something way too gold or very sequined to wear to a place to which I'll one day be invited.

Life can feel mundane but there is also *so much* beauty to capture when we consciously look for it.

## CONSIDER THIS

*Seek out simple beauty, the laughably sublime, the humor in most things, and the ridiculousness of how fleeting it all really is.*

# GIFTING HAPPINESS

Gifting is my love language and it thrills me to no end. It brings me such happiness to thoughtfully wrap presents and then watch a loved one open them, all wide eyes and smiles.

I also love receiving gifts, not because of the size or inherent value but because gifts mean thoughtfulness; they mean somebody took time out of their day to think of me. I get pangs of excitement each time I hear the chime of our doorbell for a special delivery, or when I come home to find an unexpected package on the porch. (But let us not forget the moments of sheer disappointment when I realize that the package actually just contains cat litter or dish soap, or something equally unimaginative that I've ordered and forgotten about.) Ah, life is all of the emotions—even when gifting is involved.

As a child of the 1970s and '80s, I feel a nostalgic joy to gifting that is reminiscent of finding the toy at the bottom of a sugary cereal box. It's surprising, exhilarating, and happiness-inducing. I also loved watching others excitedly pull out that toy from deep inside of the cereal; clapping with delight at a silly, brightly colored object wrapped in sealed plastic. (Though even then, I was slightly disturbed that we were supposed to eat the cereal afterward. Nothing about digging our dirty kid hands into shareable breakfast food felt sanitary. My views remain the same on this topic today . . . but I digress.)

Over the years, I've refined my love of thoughtful gifting and it has become one of my favorite pastimes. I adore witnessing the glee of a loved one opening up a long-sought-after gift. I sometimes spend months doing reconnaissance work in preparation for curating the perfect assortment of gifts. (My gifting is usually done in multiples.)

In fact, after spending the previous holiday season hiding and grieving, I made the decision to recommit to my deep love of gifting this year. I bought Ira an unsettling but highly desired sculpture made of (what looks like) human teeth and gums, set in an actual snail's shell. It is exactly as bizarre as it sounds. Apparently, it's made of resin, but you wouldn't know by looking at it. Because each piece is handmade and labor intensive, the designer has very small collections and they sell out within minutes. So in the midst of writing this manuscript and running my business, I joined the designer's mailing list, added the next collection release to my calendar, and scooped up one of her pieces as soon as the notification came through. Best gift ever. SCORE!

My brothers received overflowing bags of old-time candy, clothing, and all manner of weird items. For example, an adult-sized, neon-green fleece Grinch onesie with a faux-fur hood. It, too, is exactly as bizarre as it sounds. Apparently, the only thing that could have made it better was if it had pockets, according to my (very) adult sibling.

These offbeat but thoughtful oddities brought us days of delight.

I've also bought friends various kinds of randomness from my travels, including brightly colored slippers from India, truffle salt from France, and bags of pasta hand-carried back from Italy. I'm also not beyond sending a five-dollar "I Love NY" onesie when someone has a new baby.

Are any of these gifted items necessary? No. But are they joy-inducing and ridiculously fun? Absolutely.

I will never regret being more generous rather than less, and I am also aware of how much happiness I derive from making other people joyful. The interconnectedness of joy is palpable, so why not spread it around like colorful confetti?

## CONSIDER THIS

*Thoughtful gifts are tiny acts of kindness and generosity. They are not dictated by money (or lack thereof); they can be made, found, reused, or shared. In fact, I've found some of my favorite gifts at thrift stores, antique shops, and—when I'm very lucky—even from the Dollar Spot at Target. Allow your gifts to be in the spirit of your thoughts and the impact is so much more meaningful than simply buying that one expensive thing just because.*

# THE PLEASURE IN
## ALL THINGS

L ife is absurd and beautiful, overwhelming and mysterious, funny and tragic, thrilling and sad. And because of its vast everything-ness, I allow myself the whim of finding much delight in the simplicity of the everyday.

Deep friendships, a warm lobster roll, my cats' toes, hearing Ira's keys in the front door after a day at work, our new air fryer, the diversity of books in our local library, pink everything, a hot cup of strong coffee, inclusive conversation with new friends, my eighty-five-year-old aunt's kitchen in North Carolina, driving an orange car, brunch with girlfriends, a picture of my mom, lush green plants, my brothers' sense of humor, open spaces, holiday decorations, original hardwood flooring, my father's ability to make something out of nothing, my warm but lightweight (sleeping-bag-like) winter coat, cowboy boots, wide-leg pants, my book collection, colorful caftans, international air travel, winding conversations with loved ones, long road trips, bare shoulders in the hot summer sun, the Sunday newspaper, fresh mushrooms, the earworm music of the ice cream truck that reminds me of long hot summer days, webbed vintage lawn chairs, fresh-off-the-grill all-beef hot dogs, luxury face cream, sparkly jewelry, rose-scented body oil, all kinds of flowers, massages, freshly fallen snow, local parks, accessibility, Friday night cocktails, freedom, our fireplace, my husband's ability to fix (or make) almost anything, French doors, and built-in cabinets.

## CONSIDER THIS

*Life is absurd and overwhelming and mysterious and funny and thrilling and sad. Keeping a list of delights is a lovely reminder that the world is still a beautiful place. I find that this list is especially helpful for those moments when life feels inside out, upside down, or just plain awful.*

## PART II

# Despite Everything,
# We Are Still Here

Microjoys are accessible to us when we are present. But the paradox is that they can also occur as insights made clear only by looking backward. Microjoys ask that we find beauty in the seemingly mundane, but they also require us to hone the ability to accept life *as it is* and still find beauty wherever we are. These tiny joys live in the ordinary space of accepting and holding both this . . . and that; both past and present as truth. Like deep grief and brief moments of pure joy, or overwhelming chaos punctuated by intermittent points of calm. Tragic and peaceful. Large and small. This *and* that, at any time, can both be true.

Unavoidably, in life we will face difficulties. And

when we do, the occasional moments of observing microjoys are profound gifts that allow us the respite we
need to briefly come home to ourselves. The time to recognize that though we may be broken, we will become
whole once again. Sometimes it is within the confines
of two opposite truths that we find the deepest acts of
grace. And when that time comes, because inevitably it
will, we must learn to be in that middle space and still
allow ourselves moments of reflection and reprieve.

Many of us view the world through a simplified lens of
right or wrong, leaving little room for nuance with the
human experience. But when we do this, we miss out on
the middle space of *But. And.* We miss out on the wisdom
in knowing that we can be both happy and sad. Grieving
and joyful. Rich and poor. Angry but grateful. Microjoys
teach us to experience and accept multiple, sometimes opposite, truths at once. When we allow ourselves to simply
be in that middle space, all things can be true. And this
deep knowing is both benevolent and permission giving.
It grants us the compassion to accept joy in all forms *always*, even when life is most difficult.

The following essays are some of my own experiences

in this middle space; in the center of both this and that; microjoys born of deep grief and joy, poverty and privilege. Many of these microjoys occur as insights, appreciated only by looking backward in order to fully understand the depth of what these experiences offered. This recognition could only appear with the perspective of time. As you read these stories, I encourage you to contemplate with curiosity rather than judgment the spaces in between in your own life, past and present.

Most of us are attempting to live life *right*. But there is no one way of right-ness. Chasing one ultimate truth in most situations is an uphill battle to nowhere because so much of our existence requires holding multiple, sometimes conflicting truths. Life is rarely black and white, and the sooner we can accept nuance in every situation, the easier it becomes to navigate the life laid bare in front of us, to accept it all, as it is.

In that space of nuance and acceptance, the answer to the question of what is right or wrong depends entirely on who we ask. And my hope is that collectively, we learn to avoid seeking one right truth and instead accept that *many* things may be the most true.

These next few essays are bittersweet and were some of the most difficult for me to write. But my hope is that they remind you that microjoys (even when buried underneath the muck of the hardest things) are still available to us. They appear with the perspective of time and the wisdom of self-awareness, when we are ready to uncover and appreciate them.

**Content Warning:** Some of the essays in this section may be triggering and deal with difficult topics like illness, loss, or grief. Please take care when reading.

# FOR RICHER OR POORER

I grew up mostly happy, in relative poverty, using colorful paper food stamps to buy salty potato chips and sugary twenty-five-cent juice from the corner store and then trekking up to our second-floor apartment, belly satiated and heart full. *And.* As an adult, I've flown business class across the world (many times) and enjoyed meals that cost more than a month's rent at that childhood apartment. This *and* that. Both true. As a kid, I spent rainy summer days climbing inside of plastic milk crates so that my brothers could push me alongside the curb on our city street, my tiny vessel floating along the current of backed-up rainwater that would quickly take me down the hill on Smith Street. It was glorious and exhilarating. *And.* As an adult, I've spent lush sunny days on a steep hillside in Italy, enjoying a private pool overlooking a vast vineyard, wine in one hand and a laptop in the other. This *and* that. Both true.

With full clarity, I understand the uniqueness of my position, which exists because of, rather than in spite of, how I grew up. Living both sides of the same coin has gifted me the insight to never take my experiences for granted. And to be certain, all of these experiences are etched into the happiest places deep inside of my soul. I can still instinctively feel the delight of simpler times floating down rainwater on a city street, just as much as I can feel the deep exhale and warmth of an afternoon in the Tuscan sun.

Though some may perceive poverty as *bad* and prosperity as *good*, I know that neither is absolutely true.

That clarity has taught me to accept life *as it is* and still find joy wherever I am.

## CONSIDER THIS

*In what ways have you perceived opposites in your own life that have granted you insight and clarity? Maybe you've been inside of that place where joy got lost; where you invited guilt or shame to take center stage instead of allowing yourself the grace of respite when you needed it most. Perhaps there are (or were) moments when you accepted a situation as black and white and, in doing so, missed out on the beauty in the spectrum of the in-between.*

*The lessons that you find by looking backward may become some of your deepest microjoys, gifts of unexpected generosity bestowed upon you simply because you exist.*

# BUSY BEING BUSY

When my heart needs healing, I find ways to stay busy. The time will eventually come when I must slow down, stop, and sit inside of the heartbreak. But there are also circumstances in which busyness really is the best (temporary) medicine for what ails us.

Right after my mom died and only months after the death of my nephew, I took to painting walls, making and doing *anything* that I possibly could to avoid sitting with the hardest things. I knew the moment I sat still I would fall apart. And I also knew that I wasn't yet ready to fall apart.

On a brisk autumn day, I pulled on a thick yellow sweater and took my newspaper with me to sit at one of the outdoor tables at our local cafe. I always prefer warm weather to cool temperatures. But on that day, feeling the sharp chill in the air, holding a hot cup of coffee, seeing my palms inky from the newspaper print—it was perfection. I sat there for the rest of the afternoon, alternately talking to strangers and gazing off into nowhere.

Another day, I spent hours sanding white paint from a rusty plant stand that I found abandoned in our basement. I then painted the stand with the brightest pink (rust-proof) paint I could find. It now sits in our living room with one of Mama's plants on top. And despite my best efforts, it is collecting rust once again.

There was that month that I became fully immersed in researching tiny, strange handmade ceramics to hold small plants and cuttings. Micro oddities that should have no place in our home but somehow found a way to coexist amidst the bright colors and patterned walls anyway. Like the (slightly terrifying) one-and-a-half-inch terra-cotta face with oversized ears or the two-inch ceramic mug with a hand-carved painted hot dog on the front. These weird little vessels now hold air plants and line the living room shelves, alongside our favorite books.

There will be time to sit with the hardest things. But the respite that comes from doing, instead of sitting, is also essential. Amidst everything, these moments of contentment teach us how to hold heartbreak in one hand and stillness in the other.

**CONSIDER THIS**

*When you're struggling, gift yourself the temporary respite that comes from activity. Talk to strangers or work on small projects that offer you ease and allow your mind to wander. This wandering is not a permanent state but instead a momentary window for you to exist in peacefully within the storm. And remind yourself that—whenever it is meant to—the storm* will *pass.*

# NEW YEAR'S
# ~~RESOLUTION~~ DRESS

I now refer to 2020 as The Time That I Lived Through the Hardest Things. It shifted who I've become as an adult woman. I no longer expect that the ones I love will live forever, or that I am infallible simply because I'm healthy in this moment. I understand surrender and impermanence in ways that have cemented themselves to my bones and, also, deep inside my heart.

And. But.

Twenty-twenty was also the year that I inadvertently started my (now) favorite New Year's ritual. Days before the new year, I go shopping for a spectacular and completely unnecessary dress for absolutely no reason at all. *In spite of everything.*

It's my own private closure to the awful parts of the previous year. And it's also a statement of "HELLO, gorgeous!" toward all the microjoys to come.

These dresses don't cost a lot of money and they certainly are not the most practical items in my closet. But in light of moving through the hardest things, this small gesture is a reminder that eventually, in spite of everything, *I will be okay.*

I no longer write resolutions or choose one word to represent the next year because I've come to realize that though my hopes create an impact, I'm not actually in control of most things. So instead, I gift myself this simple pursuit, a gesture of faith in a more delightful year ahead.

How could I possibly have a horrible year while wearing a dress that is created out of fifteen pounds of gold sequins, or one that is patterned with more colors than should be legal? It's impossible not to have a good time when wearing something ridiculously over the top and completely unnecessary. (Okay, that's not quite accurate but for the sake of microjoys everywhere . . . let's go with it, shall we?)

Wear something fun and life will work out.

I mean, that's what I tell myself anyway.

**CONSIDER THIS**

*Seek out tiny joys everywhere and always choose the impractical dress. Life is too short not to.*

# AND THEN I SLEPT

My husband and I had a lovely day spent visiting a small town in rural upstate New York. We dropped in on a local bakery, one that made an incredible French pastry filled with passion fruit custard and topped with fluffy meringue. It was the kind of pastry that's so buttery and flaky it's impossible to eat with any kind of dignity. *Dignity be damned.* As I ate, pieces of flaky crust flew everywhere, including into my husband's cup of coffee.

We spent the afternoon eating local foods, perusing antique shops, and stumbling into a deep discussion with a nostalgic shopkeeper. (He seemed blissfully unaware that I was attempting to slowly inch backward out the door.) Forty-five minutes later, we emerged into sunlight once again. We walked, ate, and talked our way through the rest of the afternoon. The world outside of our own conversations fell away.

Later that evening, I dropped my husband at the nearest train station and drove myself deeper into the country for a weekend-long group retreat. I settled into my cabin, met some other attendees, and headed over to the main tent, readying myself for inspiration. It was everything I hoped it would be (except for the bugs that I determined to be *deeply* unnecessary).

Later, energized and inspired, I headed back to my cabin. I sat on the bed and out of nowhere, the waterworks began. I started to cry and I couldn't stop. Though it felt like hours, this went on for twenty (very long) minutes.

When the tears stopped flowing, I walked past the mirror and stood still. My face was so flushed and puffy that I barely recognized myself. Nose red and swollen. Eyes hollowed out with mascara-stained circles underneath. Smile lines, once smooth, were creased into deep valleys. My eyebrows were thinning and unkempt. (Weren't they fuller that afternoon?) Who was I even looking at?

There was nothing I could do to make sense of my tearful outburst except to sleep off whatever *it* was that came over me. And so, I did.

And I slept more soundly and deeply than I had in a very long time. The next morning, I woke up, refreshed and released.

Whatever *it* was, it had passed.

And with a clean face (and eyebrows as full as I remembered), I recognized myself in the mirror once again.

## CONSIDER THIS

*When you feel a tightness building in your chest, stiffness in the back of your legs, or notice that your mind keeps running even when your body is demanding that you stop, find a place where you can be calm enough to release whatever it is that you've held on to for too long, whether it's been days, weeks, or decades.*

## WHEN GRATITUDE
## IS ENOUGH

As I slowly began to reemerge from the darkness, a semblance of the life I'd formerly known began to take hold once again. A life of tiny pleasures and big accomplishments: dinner with neighbors, yoga outdoors, cocktails on the waterfront, a book deal with my ideal publisher (for this book!), and even the gift of a brand-new shiny orange car from my in-laws. Joy. Triumph. Delight. Life is almost . . . wonderful. Almost.

These were the moments when the haze started to lift

and the sun could slowly peek through once again after a long spell of darkness. These moments afforded me the chance to momentarily recognize myself from the Before Times; myself from the forty-three years prior. Myself as I once was before the hardest things happened.

But I am different now.

Though I can intuit and understand how incredible all of these moments are, I cannot yet celebrate them without feeling performative. Me, a woman who once celebrated Every. Tiny. Thing. To celebrate, I must first be able to feel deeply again, and right now, I don't. I feel some things some of the time but mostly, my feelings have dulled—they simply aren't as sharp as they once were. They are no longer technicolor but instead mostly monochromatic. I am here. But not quite, not yet.

I do still feel life *in color*. Just differently, at least for now. And so an exaggerated celebration of wins, regardless of how big or small, is not in the imminent future. And that is okay.

I may choose to throw a giant party someday and celebrate my reemergence from living through the hardest things. But not today. Today, I will acknowledge these beautiful experiences, tiny wins, and huge accomplishments with a bow of gratitude but not yet with a celebration. And the grace that I've given myself by appreciating what *is* without attaching an insincere celebration, that freedom is an enormous* microjoy. One that I can only recognize by coming through the other side of living through the hardest things.

## CONSIDER THIS

*Consider how you move through difficult times (difficult doesn't have to mean the hardest things). What habits are you continuing to nurture that*

---

* Remember: Not all microjoys are small. Many are big, bold, and audacious, but they're also readily available when we are not able to reach very far to discover them.

*may not serve you anymore? What actions are you taking that you may be better served to leave behind, even temporarily? What small grace do you need to extend to yourself instead? You don't always have to be all things to everyone, including to yourself.*

# MUNDANE WEEKEND
# MORNINGS

I cherish the normalcy of a slow Saturday morning. Wearing long flowy satin pajama pants that trail the floor, I make my way (not gracefully) to our kitchen to pour a cup of coffee. Mug in one hand, I open the front door to pick up our weekend paper. Not yet fully awake, I pull out the real estate and metropolitan (and sometimes cooking) sections of *The New York Times* and toss the rest onto the sofa next to me.

Ira goes right in for the hard stuff: black coffee in

hand, feet firmly rooted to the floor, readying himself to peruse the thick front section of the paper. And in weird opposition to the heaviness of front-page news, our tiny orange cat flops around in the background, playing with a jingling felt mouse. (Side note: Why do we continue buying these absurdly annoying cat toys? Because we love these damn cats, that's why.)

After having spent much of the previous year in and out of hospital waiting rooms and unconsciously waiting for phone calls that no one deserves to receive, my husband and I both have deep gratitude for unremarkable weekend mornings.

In fact, it was ironically on a quiet Saturday morning that my mother FaceTimed and told me to take a deep breath and sit down. With as much calm as she could muster, she spoke what must have been some of the hardest words she'd ever say out loud: my nephew, her first grandchild, was killed the night before.

I sat, stunned, silent.

After ending the call, I immediately dialed her back

". . . Mom. Are they sure he's not alive? I mean, isn't it possible that he might be?" Always the optimist; the memory of that conversation is seared into my soul.

Earlier that morning—while I had obliviously sat cross-legged in meditation—my mother, ever protective of my heart, rang Ira to ask if he could drive me back to my family home. Considering that we'd visited the day before, she knew I'd be worried if I didn't have an explanation for another trip back. And Ira knew that I wouldn't go anywhere without one. So by the time I'd gotten off the call, he'd already packed food and an overnight bag for the drive back.

My brother was the first person I saw, and I immediately collapsed onto the sidewalk in front of him. I sat on the ground, childlike, looking up at him. "I am just so sorry, big brother. I can't believe that this is true." "I know, sis. I know." He reached down, pulled me up, and hugged me close before I went inside to see my mother.

That unfathomable moment feels like a part of

someone else's Saturday morning from a million life-times ago.

Sixteen months later, on a similarly mundane Saturday morning, I sit on our blush-colored sofa surrounded by plants, sunlight, and lounging cats.

The pleasure of a boring weekend morning will never again be lost on me.

### CONSIDER THIS

*When you are in the depths of your own hardest things, please,* please *remind yourself that this,* whatever it is, *will eventually pass. It will not change what is, nor will it bring back those that we love, or undo the hard things that have already been done. But this time, this moment, this experience, this awful, shitty thing . . . it will eventually pass. And somehow, by the grace of someone or something greater than us, you* will *find a new way forward.*

# BETTER. ENOUGH.

Who I am has never been quite enough (for me). I've assigned myself the seemingly endless task of attempting to constantly become a better version of myself, a better version of who I was even moments before: a more worthy friend, a more inspiring teacher, a less self-absorbed writer, a more self-aware human. I've spent four decades trying to become better while also attempting to make other people feel loved, seen, and appreciated. And just for good measure, I've also spent at least half of that time simultaneously seeking out the perfect shade of bright pink nail polish. (Because how could I possibly become a better human without the perfect shade of bright pink polish?)

The truth is, after losing so much so quickly, I'm no longer interested in becoming anything other than who I *already* am. A grown woman who is trying to figure out how to move through her days once again, a friend who is sometimes present and lately more absent, a wife who is trying to connect but is often separate, and a teacher who has temporarily stopped teaching. I have nothing left to give and who I am is all I have. I cannot *become* . . . any more.

And so, I look in the mirror and think: "This is it. Right now, I am all that I will ever be in this world. I've somehow made it to this point, as this exact woman that I am. And even if I never find that perfect shade of pink nail polish, somehow I will still be okay."

At least momentarily. At least for today.

## CONSIDER THIS

*When you're done becoming better and you get to that bottomless place where you have nothing left to offer, know that there really is nothing more you need to do (except perhaps, if you're lucky, continue looking for that perfect shade of bright pink nail polish).*

# AUTUMN BBQ

Instead of my usual *doing*, I've recently been spending a lot of my time learning, listening, praying, and quietly writing. After years of having an on-and-off meditation practice, I'm back on. Today is day twenty, and though my mind rarely stays completely still, I sit anyway. It's been fourteen months since my mama passed away. And though I sense her presence every day, I feel especially connected with her through meditation. Maybe my connection to her is the reason I continue to sit in meditation daily.

While packing for a recent trip, I thought of Mom

and pulled out a collage of photos that I made of her and my nephew. I listened to her voice on a recording from a few months before she passed. When it was over, I said out loud, "Mom, I miss you. Can you show me if you're still around?" I continued packing. Continued moving. Continued doing. Until my phone rang a few minutes later.

My brother called to tell me about the strangest thing that had just happened. While he was grilling pork chops in the backyard, he stepped away. And then completely forgot about his dinner. He got distracted. For fifteen minutes, with three burners on high heat, he left the pork chops cooking on the grill.

When he suddenly remembered his dinner, he fully expected that, in addition to a small grill fire that might need tending, the pork chops would be burnt to a crisp.

Except. They weren't.

They were perfectly cooked. Exceptionally cooked, even. And on a cool but windless autumn day, every single burner was turned off.

*Every. Single. One.*

No one else was around.

I asked my brother when this had happened.

". . . fifteen minutes ago."

Almost exactly the moment that I asked Mom to show me if she was still with us.

## CONSIDER THIS

*In good conscience, I have to acknowledge that connecting more deeply to those who've passed on is contingent on your own beliefs and intuition. You must trust what is true and genuine for you. For me, meditation and spending time in quiet contemplation help to bridge the gap between this world and (what I believe to be) the next. If that feels honest and authentic to you, I invite you to try either or both. And if it doesn't align with you, know that you can find your own ways to feel* connected to loved ones. Some people write letters, create an altar, pray, visit their loved one's favorite places, or even continue to share stories aloud about them as a form of connection. Regardless of what you try, I hope you find a way that feels most genuine to you.

# SMALL MERCIES

It's been almost a year since I was diagnosed with early-stage breast cancer. Almost seven months since the final drive of twenty-eight consecutive days of radiation treatments. Amidst so much loss, being diagnosed came as *just one more* thing to be dealt with. I remember feeling that my life was like an oncoming train that I couldn't stop. And so, I didn't try to stop it. I simply surrendered. Because that was all that I could summon the energy to do.

The first preinvasive cancer cells were found during my annual mammogram. I had never felt any lumps, so I'd been expecting a clean bill of health. Receiving that first phone call felt like I was sideswiped. I remember my thoughts vacillating between "Is this a fucking joke?! How is this even possible right now?" and the ever optimistic "It could be worse, we caught it early! At least we're near one of the best cancer hospitals in the world!" and, in my most humbling moments, "Yes, of course this could happen to me. Why should I be immune to this train wreck? This is life and I'm not special. Let's just do the damn thing and keep on moving."

After additional scans, a second spot with cancer was found. I was in the middle of getting a pedicure when I got the call from my oncologist. (Yes, I was getting my toenails painted and answered a call from the hospital. I still don't know why I picked up right then. Either way, I did.) I recall nodding quietly and saying that I understood, even while the oncologist prompted me to ask more questions. I had no questions because there was nothing that I could do to change *what was true*. I had cancer; that was the truth. That was *the only truth* in that moment. What else did I really need to ask?

After moving to a different state, reeling from the murder of my nephew, the sudden death of my mother, and the near death of my sibling in an eight-month period *while in the midst of a global pandemic*, I had no emotional bandwidth to feel anything. All I could do was put one foot in front of the other.

And from that place of full surrender, we scheduled the surgery and then planned for radiation treatments beginning six weeks later. Each morning, I'd wake up at 7:00 a.m., take a shower, get in the car, turn on my audiobook, arrive at the hospital, undress, go for the (approximately) fifteen-minute radiation sessions, get dressed again, drive to the nearby Dunkin' Donuts for coffee and avocado toast before driving myself back home. Day in and day out. Until it was over.

I told very few people about my diagnosis. In the months leading up to it, I'd experienced enough sympathy and kindness to last several lifetimes. I didn't want to be the person requiring pity nor did I want to be perceived as being incapable of handling life's hardships. And so, I told only my husband, mother-in-law, and a few close friends. To this day, I still have yet to tell my brothers. (Before this book is published, I will tell them. I promise.)

In hindsight, I consider the timing of my diagnosis to be a small mercy. I've grappled with anxiety through most of my adulthood. But because so much was happening all at once, it allowed me to move through it all without the added weight of my tendency to overthink and under-sleep. All I could do was surrender because there really was *no other way*. And that was a much-needed mercy, indeed.

**CONSIDER THIS**

*In our most difficult moments, having the ability to surrender takes self-awareness because you are called to let go of situations that you cannot influence. You accept that you really are* not in control.

*You accept that whether you actively push and pull or sit and wait, the outcome will not likely change. Having the ability to surrender takes an inner knowing that this, too, shall pass. When you come up against the world and yourself, when there is no other way out, consider moving through by surrendering. The phrase that often comes to mind is this: let go and let God.*

# THE THANKSGIVING AFTER

When I was growing up, my mother prepared home-cooked dinners on most nights. Dinner usually included meat or fish, a starch, and a vegetable (canned or frozen was the norm). If we were really lucky, there would also be dessert—perhaps a graham-cracker-crust apple Betty with Cool Whip on top. Even after I became an adult, my mother still held on to this standard of what a meal *should* include. Whenever I'd say that we were cooking dinner, she'd not-so-subtly interrogate me about any missing components of her self-proclaimed food pyramid. (Because apparently starch would "put hair on our chest" and vegetables would make us strong "like Popeye." By this time, I was well into adulthood and the likelihood of ever becoming "strong like Popeye" was slim to none. Also, I didn't want hair on my chest and we don't really know how to cook meat properly. But my mother thought it was funny so she kept using the same lines to try to get me to change my cooking habits.)

Mom loved to feed her family and every Thanksgiving she would start preparing the meal days in advance. There was no other food to be cooked in the kitchen leading up to Thanksgiving dinner, so we'd spend the day hungry while we waited. By night's end, we'd have a huge turkey, a tray of chopped BBQ, and a medium-sized roast beef, too. And sometimes an entire chicken if someone was stopping by that didn't like turkey. (I mean, who really likes turkey, anyway?) Oh, and also stuffing (the starch!), creamed spinach, candied carrots, a giant pot of collard greens with more pork, sweet potato rings with pineapple (more starch!), sweet potato mash (even more starch!), six to eight homemade coconut cream pies, two homemade chocolate mousse pies, one large homemade apple pie, plus store-bought lemon meringue, pecan, and pumpkin pies, too. Mom prepared a feast every year because, to her, food was love.

As her health declined, the rest of us took a more active part in preparing the Thanksgiving meal. We didn't necessarily want to, because in doing so, we knew that we were also acknowledging that her health was failing. And that acknowledgment was a form of anticipatory grieving that we weren't ready for.

But whether we were ready or not, Mom passed away at the end of September. As the first holiday season without her approached, we were deep into grieving the loss of my nephew and my mother. And it was also during that same time that my sibling was admitted into the ICU, first with a stroke . . . and then heart failure. My husband, my oldest brother, and I (along with my mom's dog) spent that Thanksgiving somberly sitting on my sofa watching TV, waiting for the other shoe to drop, during what already felt like the worst year possible.

One year later, life was slowly showing a semblance of normalcy again. My aforementioned sibling was now home and recovering from heart surgery. Thirteen months had passed since Mom died, and seventeen months since my nephew's death. We needed to ground in some form of family tradition. And it was from that place that we decided that we'd collectively replicate the Thanksgiving dinners from our past. Three adult siblings and a husband could absolutely remake the meal that my mom cooked for forty-plus years, right? Erhm, no. No, we couldn't. But nonetheless, we tried.

We attempted to make sweet potato rings. My oldest brother insisted he could make them without looking at the recipe. My other brother and I looked on in disbelief while laughing out loud at how wrong it was going. After much drama about whether or not tapioca was really necessary in the recipe and if the vegan marshmallows that my husband picked up (Ira, c'mon!) could even melt, the sweet potato rings actually did turn out okay. My other brother, together with my husband, tried his hand at a ten-pound rotisserie turkey and a roasted lemon chicken, too. If I'm being really honest, their turkey was some of the best I'd ever had—the crispy skin was just the right amount of savory with fresh herbs and the meat was almost decadent in moistness and flavor. Mama would've been very proud.

I, on the other hand, went for the most difficult of all of the recipes to replicate: our family's legendary coconut cream pie. This is, I believe, my grandmother's recipe and it takes hours to prepare. There are lots of moving parts that include hardening and remelting gelatin at just the right temperature and whipping (but making sure not to overwhip!) the cream. I am not a pie-maker; I've accepted that I will never be a pie-maker. But. And. I spent hours that day attempting to make eight of these pies. Somehow, I got the measurements wrong and made at least double the ingredients that were needed, and the gelatin decidedly was not behaving as it should have, either. But I stuck it out because I was committed (*and the ingredients cost a small fortune*). After hours of effort and throwing away half of the prepared ingredients, the pies were finally finished.

In the end, they turned out (erhm) kind of but not really sort of okay-ish. They weren't delicious but they weren't awful, either, so we considered that a win.

We set the dining table, placed pictures of Mom and my nephew at the head, and celebrated cooking and laughing together once again. But mostly, we celebrated what a blessing it is to have a legacy of tradition and the deep knowing that food really is love (even when it isn't perfect).

## CONSIDER THIS

*As my mother's health was beginning to decline, in lieu of holiday or birthday gifts, I asked that she handwrite our family recipes. I knew that we had family cookbooks and recipes typed up and strewn about, but I really wanted to have them in my mother's own hand. She spent the following year doing just that. She bought a blank recipe book and wrote down as many recipes as she could. And alongside the recipes, she also gave me motherly advice (e.g., "Don't walk away from the stove while . . ." or "Be careful not to burn the bottom," etc.). Every time I open the cookbook, I am enveloped by my mom's love. I don't know how I had the foresight to ask for this gift but I am grateful that I did.*

*While your loved ones are present and alive, ask them to share their wisdom and traditions with you in their own handwriting. You can treasure these and pass them on, creating a beautiful legacy of food, love, and tradition. (I'm a sentimentalist and appreciate the written word but typed recipes and traditions are equally valuable. And depending on one's handwriting, possibly even preferable for ease of reading later.)*

*Traditions and recipes are challenging to replicate when our loved ones die. But new traditions with a similar intention of love, kindness, inclusion, etc. are always possible—like a recipe that is amended and becomes different but equally delicious with each iteration. Regardless of whether your loved ones are biological or chosen, and regardless of whether they've left written notes, you can always create your own traditions and new recipes that will one day become a part of your own legacy.*

# SUMMER FRIDAYS
# IN THE CITY

On a Friday after our move to the suburbs, Ira and I rented a hotel room in New York City and made plans with friends that we hadn't seen in over a year. We met a friend on our hotel rooftop at 4:00 p.m. and enjoyed delightful summer cocktails against a backdrop of the most spectacular city views. It was busy but not crowded; it was loud, boisterous, and ridiculously happy in a way that I've only experienced on post-work summer Fridays in New York City. I think it's the excitement of feeling free, purposeful, and alive in one of the most interesting cities in the world (in my humble opinion, of course). Most people who live in New York City aren't originally from there, and the energy and enthusiasm for their adopted home is visceral.

Even now, when I no longer have a traditional job to escape from at 1:00 p.m. on Fridays, I find few things as magical as the (sometimes) chic debauchery of a fancy New York rooftop when it's eighty degrees outside. There's this stark opposition of concrete, high-rise buildings, and rushing people to the relaxing summer vibe of being thirty floors above it all while sipping a beautiful libation and eating mouthwatering nibbles (*that cost more than dinner anywhere else in the country.* But I digress).

While many people escape the city during the summer, Ira and I have always been so fond of it. It's less busy, the pace is slower, and there seems to be more available green space in many areas. (Some friends strongly disagree and insist that summer in the city is stuffy, smells like hot garbage, and becomes unbearable. But we are not focusing on those friends right now.)

Back to this particular summer evening. After a slight delay at the bar, our gorgeous bartender offered us a complimentary round of drinks. Actually, the bartender didn't *offer* them so much as graciously brought them over to our table without consent. Considering that we were wrapping up to head to an event farther downtown, we set out to find other friendly rooftop-goers to give them to. Cocktails on an NYC rooftop are *not* inexpensive and so the gratitude extended from this offer was palpable. We were thrilled, the receivers of the drinks were happy, and off we went, in the same jovial spirit in which we'd arrived a few hours prior.

**CONSIDER THIS**

*I've experienced moments similar to this many times throughout my adulthood in New York City, and still I feel such a thrill. I don't take for granted that life will always be so carefree and joyous; in* fact, I know that it won't be. These beautiful moments are fleeting and will end as quickly as they began. And so I hold them as they happen. I observe them in real time, slowly savor them, and let them go when they end, knowing that I now have a reserve of delightful memories to hold on to.

There is so much nuance in the details. Notice them. Delight in them. Hear the sounds around you and observe life even in the most mundane of scenarios, whether walking through your neighborhood, perusing at a library, or sipping coffee at a local cafe. There is so much more than what initially meets the eye.

# MOTHER LOVE

*The deeper that sorrow carves into your being,*
*the more joy you can contain.*

—Kahlil Gibran

I don't think I will ever *not* miss my mother. She was a force. And I am my mother's daughter, through and through. But as time passes, sometimes in the midst of normalcy, I find that I'm doing okay. Not always, but sometimes.

I wonder if it's partially because there were no words

left unspoken. I've always said the things I wanted her to know: *the good* ("I am the woman you are proud of today because of what you perceive to be your shortcomings as a mother. Through your example, you taught me resilience, love, and forgiveness. Don't forget that, Mom."), *the random* ("Did you know that potatoes went up to four dollars per pound? I think we're going to have to stop eating soon!"), and *the awful* ("Oh, for the love of God, Mom! I just spoke to you an hour ago, nothing has changed since then, why are you calling me again?!").

She taught me to communicate clearly, to speak my mind even when I was afraid to, but maybe most importantly, to always acknowledge my feelings. And because of this, I spent a lifetime communicating honestly (mostly*) with my mother.

We spoke every day and we argued *all the time*. Like I said, she taught me to always acknowledge my

---

\* She didn't need to know *everything*, she was still my mother. Geezus!

feelings, and I took full advantage of this in our relationship. And. But. Neither of us ever questioned how much we loved each other. (Okay, maybe there were moments of Jewish mom guilt where she tested the "You don't love me" tactic, but it never worked.) She knew I loved her.

Though her death was the most difficult experience I've lived through, there weren't any words left unsaid. I was there as she was dying, and she is still here now. Different but present.

The relationship that we had as mother and adult daughter was often a complicated but also divinely privileged one. And how lucky that, in this lifetime, I was given my larger-than-life, potty-mouthed, big-hearted mother for forty-three whole imperfect years.

Grieving and mourning sucks.* Full stop. And. But.

......................................

* As I understand it, grief and mourning are *not* the same. Grief is deeply personal and refers to the *internal* thoughts and feelings that we have preceding or following the loss of a loved one (heartache, sadness, anger, etc.). Grief isn't necessarily displayed publicly. Mourning, on the other hand, is the *external* expression of our loss that helps us to create long-term

The love I shared with my mother somehow makes mourning her worthwhile, more doable. It feels to me like a balancing of the scales between how much we grieve and how much we love—I don't have a logical explanation for this. Accepting her loss and choosing to move forward doesn't make accepting her death easier, but honoring that my feelings of loss are equal to the love we shared allows me to keep going. My friend, the writer Marisa Renee Lee, whose mother also died, says that grief is love. I believe this. We sometimes feel grief in relation to how much we feel love.

I'll never not miss my mother. But because of her love, I will—unsteadily, and with courage—learn how to move forward once again.

........................................................................................

memories about what or whoever we've lost (holding a memorial, sharing stories, crying, keeping pictures nearby, writing about them, etc.). Writing some of these essays is how I mourn my loved ones. It is how I outwardly grieve. I believe that we can mourn our losses for a lifetime and *still* find joy and happiness in the present.

## CONSIDER THIS

*Communicate clearly, even when you're afraid to speak your mind. And most importantly, when you love someone, tell them. Often.*

# A PANDEMIC
# JOURNAL ENTRY FOR
# DIFFICULT TIMES

I wrote a version of this entry during the early days of the pandemic, while most of us were confined within our homes, but these words still hold true, years later.

It's day seventy-four of isolation and I'm exasperated. I don't want to count any more days or weeks or months. I simply want to get on with life, whatever this new life will look like. You, too, perhaps?

Feelings have run the gamut: confusion, gratitude, joy, surrender, anger, sadness, moments of happiness, then grief, and finally, back to confusion. Over and over again. All felt while baking, practicing yoga, puzzling, cooking, face masking, sitting, meditating, and hell, even online shopping. *What a time.*

But also.

We must continue. One foot and then the other until those steps begin to feel like our own again, lighter and more balanced. We have to hold on to hope. To believe that things will get better, because they will. To hope for brighter days, brighter hours, and brighter moments. For a time when we can hug our friends and kiss our loved ones freely, without concern. For a time when the world feels kinder, gentler, and more accepting. For the moments when we can smile at a stranger without a face mask. For a time when we can simply breathe in the fresh air around us, while in the community of others. For a time when folks can run around freely outside regardless of the color of their skin or the language that they speak.

These days will come. They must. Because we will

not give up hope. We cannot give up hope; it's the *one* thing that will save us all.

We will get there.

**CONSIDER THIS**

*This difficult moment is a blip, a drop, a teeny-tiny grain of sand in a great big world. That doesn't make what we've been through any less painful. We are changed. We've shed tears. We've shed layers of our former selves. We've lost people that we love. We may always miss what used to be. And. Still. We will emerge, more tender and fragile, but also more resilient, courageous, and (hopefully) kind. But before that can happen, we must allow time to help us grieve and heal before we renew once again.*

# ON TWOSDAY

On a random Tuesday night in February, I couldn't fall asleep.

When I experience bouts of insomnia, I watch an episode of something undemanding on my iPad. When I'm feeling nostalgic, I'll watch reruns of 1970s and '80s sitcoms. When I'm feeling less nostalgic, my go-to show is an animated comedy called *Bob's Burgers*. (Go ahead and judge me. And. Or. Watch an episode yourself and see if the absurd humor lulls you into relaxation as well. It really is ridiculously silly.)

As I said, on this random Tuesday night in February,

I couldn't sleep—but apparently the day wasn't as random as I'd presumed.

I have no experience with numerology, but many of those who do believe that good things come in twos, so this particular Tuesday was auspicious: 2.22.22. Several numerologists forecasted that the day would help us to reflect on how we communicate with our loved ones while supporting us in maintaining a more open-hearted connection. For no particular reason, I avoided social media most of that day, and so I missed much of the online chatter about the day's significance. But as I was struggling to fall asleep at 11:11 p.m., I opened my iPad to watch a show. I connected my AirPods* and this appeared on the screen: "Chelley's AirPods."

Except. *They were not.*

Chelley is my mom and she passed away on 9.22.20. Seventeen months before . . . *to the day.*

................................................

\* I use the terms "AirPods" and "earbuds" interchangeably throughout this essay.

My mom never owned AirPods. Truthfully, she wouldn't have known what to do with them if she did. *I know this* because I bought her a bright pink, easy-to-use headset the year before she became sick. (It was the kind with a mouthpiece microphone that makes the wearer look like a switchboard operator from the early 1900s. It was fantastic!)

But I digress.

I bought the AirPods I was currently using long after Mom passed away. And still.

For no explainable reason, at exactly 11:11 p.m., her name appeared on my tablet screen.

Since the day I purchased them, these have been programmed as "Cyndie's AirPods." I picked up my phone from the nightstand and, using Bluetooth, tried to connect to my earbuds. As always, they appeared as "Cyndie's AirPods."

I then connected them back to my iPad and *once again*, saw these words appear: "Chelley's AirPods."

In life, my mom was never one for subtlety and

apparently, *she still isn't*. Clearly, she wants my AirPods. And then I recall that I never did see her use that bright pink headset anyway . . . and now I know why.

**CONSIDER THIS**

*I don't know how this happened; I also don't feel a need to question it. With full integrity, I can't confirm that this was not a strange technical glitch, nor do I think it's important. Is non-questioning simply a form of blind faith on my part? Desperate hopefulness? Extreme optimism? A physical need to stay connected to my loved ones? Perhaps all of this is true, even likely. But so what?!*

*What I do know is that I've continued to nurture my relationship with loved ones who have passed away. I have an altar. I keep pictures throughout our home. I light candles in front of their pictures when I hope to actively channel their* support and love. I speak to them out loud. I've become attuned to the subtleties of how it makes me feel to believe that they are still around me; I feel better, more safe, and comforted. I am their legacy. Particularly after my mother died, I've felt a deep calling to continue to stay in communication.

If that feels genuine to you, I invite you to do the same. And if it doesn't, then don't.

But either way, stay in alignment with your own integrity and connect in ways that make you feel better, safer, and more comforted in life . . . and in loss.

# A GIRL-CHILD
# IN STILETTO HEELS

A picture memory from fourteen years ago popped up in my email inbox. It was me at thirty years old—wild curls, wide-eyed, and all smiles—leaning cheek to cheek with an ex-boyfriend against the backdrop of a dimly lit Lower East Side bar.

He was a French actor and producer seven years my senior who split his time between New York City and Paris. (Let's call him Jean.) I was working full-time in the New York fashion industry, but traveled back and forth to France to see him when he was filming. The relationship was expansive, beautiful, and sexy but, also, extremely volatile. No. Actually, in that relationship, I *felt* expansive, beautiful, and sexy but, also, extremely volatile. In hindsight, I felt like a girl-child trying to walk in stiletto heels. I didn't know how to be in an adult relationship because I didn't know who I was as an adult at that point in my life. My father had passed away two years prior. I was freshly out of an eight-year romantic relationship. And I was at the height of working long hours while also enjoying my newfound life as a New Yorker.

By the time I met Jean, I was mostly oblivious to everyone else around me as I traveled and spent my time exploring all the city had to offer: late-night piano bar sing-alongs, full court access to Mick Jagger at a Rolling Stones concert, beautiful daytime cocktails, and all kinds of fantastic debauchery. It was a weird and wonderful time. In hindsight, I credit that era *including* my relationship with Jean for the journey that led me to become the woman I am today.

Within the almost two years that Jean and I dated, I formed a wider understanding of the world around me. I became a more sophisticated, grown-up version of myself. I no longer felt like *just* a girl from New Jersey who was trying to understand where I belonged. Instead, I stretched and evolved into a young woman who came to better understand simple beautiful food, fine wine, the complexity of relationships, weird art, and beauty in ways that were nontraditional for someone from my (very humble) upbringing. I learned of a world that I didn't have access to before him, a bohemian one where creatives seamlessly moved back and forth between major cities throughout the world, crafted interesting work, prepared massive meals with overflowing bottles of wine for friends, and slept until noon each day. I had no idea where anyone's money came from or how they afforded this lifestyle; this giant new world was wide open and foreign to me. Until then, I mostly tried to stand out while also fitting in. I worked a nine-to-six (ish) job, wore the "right" clothing, attempted to appear interesting enough, and tried to be as cool as I could be. Again, a girl-child in stiletto heels, wandering the streets of New York.

The relationship with Jean ended horribly—not because he was bad and I was good or vice versa. It ended because we exhausted what it should have been at that stage in my life; we overstayed our welcome in a relationship that should have ended six months after it began.

Fourteen years later, it is still humbling to write about our breakup. Like a scene out of a television sitcom, I came home after work to our newly rented West Village apartment to find it empty of all of his belongings. After an argument the night before, I'd asked him to leave. I didn't think he actually would. (Only months prior, he'd packed up his entire life in Paris, including his dog, and moved to New York for me. For us.) As I said, it ended horribly. And. But.

That relationship became the impetus for my lifelong commitment to therapy and self-awareness. I discovered quickly that I had a lot to learn on my own before I could invite anyone else in. I spent years in therapy getting clear about my behaviors and their impact while tearfully and exhaustively working through my own lifelong shit. (I also learned what it meant to pay full NYC rent on my own dime!)

I dated casually after Jean but, truly, the lessons learned from that relationship are largely responsible for the happiness that I share with my grounded, loving, stylish (and very attractive) husband today.*

Had I not done the work that this breakup led me to, I could never sustain the wide-open, communicative, and deeply loving relationship that Ira and I share with each other. By the time we met in our late thirties, we'd both been in therapy and worked on ourselves as individuals, physically and emotionally. We'd each been in less than stellar relationships with perfectly fine people.

........................................................

* When writing an essay dedicated to how a former relationship supported your growth, the right thing to do is to highly compliment your current partner in ways that they absolutely deserve. *Hi, gorgeous Ira.*

We learned, stretched, overstretched, grew, and evolved into the responsible grown-ups that we are today.

And if not for the difficult lessons that I learned as a girl-child in high heels wandering the streets of New York City while getting my heart broken into a thousand little pieces, I might not be in the profoundly loving relationship that I have with my husband.

## CONSIDER THIS

*Breakups, breakdowns, loneliness, and perceived failures—these are some of the in-between times that show us who we truly are. The most profound lessons and blessings are often earned during the time in between spent trudging, running, or scaling as we find our way up or back down the mountain of uncertainty that is life. Pay close attention to all of these magnificent moments, the good and the awful—there are a whole lot of lessons (and blessings) awaiting you.*

# TIME IS AN ASSHOLE.*
# WEAR THE GOWN.

With nowhere at all to go, I recently put on a gown—not a *dress* but a *floor-sweeping gown*—with pockets and a light crinoline underneath for extra pouf. It was the gown that I meant to wear for a friend's wedding in the English countryside during Labor Day weekend, 2019. We had to cancel because it was the same weekend my mom initially became sick. She went into septic shock just as

--------------------------------------------------

* Dear reader, please don't allow this language to distract you from this hard-won wisdom. Time really is a complete and utter asshole and I could think of no better word to describe this.

Ira and I were headed to pick her up for a weekend away, some time together before we left for England. Or so we thought.

Life has been a whirlwind ever since, and only recently have things begun to settle down, three years later. In hindsight, initially getting Mom such immediate care bought us another year with her in this lifetime. And for that I am forever very grateful because that time was more precious than we could've ever known.

Mom first got sick in late August. She was in the hospital and rehab through late October. In fact, she spent her seventieth birthday in rehabilitation. We tried to make it a happy one, but the dark walls and atmosphere of sickness all around us made it harder to keep up the act. Still, she was alive. And for the most part, her illness was manageable. She was in rehab only to finish out a strong dose of antibiotics. She was over the moon to be returning home once she was done. Mom always ran the show and did that best from her own home. Of course, my surly mom ended up becoming dear friends with all of the rehabilitation staff—but only after she initially cussed them out while laying out her boundaries for care while she was there. (*That* is my mother, in a nutshell.) Before she left the facility, they brought her cards and treats and also told her that they never wanted to see her there again. She agreed.

None of us could have known what the year ahead would bring. We buried Mom on her seventy-first birthday.

Which brings me back to wearing an unnecessary gown and a full face of makeup for our Dear Grown Ass Women Zoom soiree.*

We don't know how much time we have. We don't know when, or if, illness will strike without warning. And we are not guaranteed even one more day to be present for the ones we love.

The past few years taught me a whole lot. But one of

---

* Dear Grown Ass Women is a beloved community that I founded in 2019; you should absolutely join us.

the most important lessons I've learned is that time is an asshole who moves swiftly.

As cliché as this may sound, I can say with full confidence that all we truly have is *this exact moment*. And when our time comes (or that of our loved ones) to leave this world behind, nothing else will matter. Not owning a new car, getting that fancy promotion, publishing a bestseller, or being the coolest kid on the block. NOTHING ELSE WILL MATTER. You will break down and fall apart at the seams. Life will cloud over and never be as bright again. You will unlearn everything about yourself that you once thought was true. You will feel like you are walking through molasses. You will forget who you were and barely recognize yourself except for pictures taken from the times before.

And. But. With each day that passes, you will pick up those teeny, tiny shards of the life you used to know. *You will heal*, and some days will move you forward while others shift you ten steps backward. And though you will never be the same, as the art of kintsukuroi* teaches us, you may become just a bit more resilient, courageous, and beautiful *because you were broken*. You will be okay once again, and life will continue on.

## CONSIDER THIS

*Loss is a surefire way of remembering our relation-ship to time, but it is not the only way to become more present. How might your behaviors and ac-tions shift if you* really *acknowledged that time is our most limited resource? What might you do*

........................................

* In *A Year of Positive Thinking*, I defined kintsukuroi: "Kintsukuroi is a kind of Japanese ceramic style . . . meaning 'to repair with gold.' In the kintsuku-roi tradition, when a ceramic piece breaks, an artisan will fuse the pieces back together using liquid gold or gold-dusted lacquer. So rather than being covered up, the breaks become more obvious, and a new piece of art emerges from the brokenness. Kintsukuroi embraces flaws and imperfection, but it also teaches the essence of resilience. Every crack in a ceramic piece is part of its history, and each piece becomes more beautiful because it has been broken."

*differently? What might you continue to do? In*
*what ways might your perspective shift? Logically*
*we know that time waits for no one, but cultivat-*
*ing a practice of checking in with yourself around*
*how you spend your time reinforces this reality in*
*ways that offer deeper reflection and self-awareness.*

# PART III

# Becoming Enough: Relationships with Ourselves and Others

Relationships are at the center of our lives. They carve deep, indelible marks into our soul. When we observe microjoys through the lens of human connection, life becomes magnified. Vital to this experience is an understanding of the deeper truths and nuances of the human condition. In our formative years, we have no understanding of the complexity of ourselves or others. But in time, we come to realize that we are all equal parts brokenhearted and whole, tended to and abandoned, ambiguous and clear, exposed and protected.

Relationships are varied, from lifelong friendships to beloved pets, from our biological family to the folks we meet briefly over the course of our lives. They all matter.

When we take the time to consider how they each impact us, we become kinder and more empathetic. And that kindness extends to the most essential relationship that we will ever cultivate: the one that we form with ourselves.

This relationship is always evolving, changing as we shift, bend, stretch, break, heal, and grow throughout our lifetime. There will be times that we move through the world feeling uncertain, and there will be times that we have moments of crystal clarity and overwhelming confidence. All of it is true and much of it is centered around our relationships.

Who we were yesterday matters as much as who we will become tomorrow. And when we learn to release self-judgment and accept all the parts of who we are, we appreciate the profound wisdom that resides below the surface of our being.

Through cultivating diverse relationships, we begin to unravel our truest selves while also understanding how much more alike we are than different. It is often from our daily interactions that we reveal our innermost sense of belonging, and sometimes our insecurity.

But perhaps, through all of these interactions, we may also witness our most intense microjoys; those that rise from the deepest space within our souls. Those that elevate, educate, and equip us to become the most discerning and enlightened versions of ourselves.

# METAMORPHOSIS

It was a frigid day in the middle of December and life was incredibly quiet. It felt like the devastating calm after a turbulent, disturbing storm. It was the kind of year that actually caused a beloved friend to sheepishly ask this question: "Cyndie, do you think you're cursed?" Oof. I certainly hoped not but I couldn't fault her for suggesting it. It had been a hell of a year, indeed.

But somehow on that frigid mid-December day, I was more present and focused than I'd been in a very long time. I could sit down without feeling jittery. I could finally hear myself think without the constant buzzing of thoughts raging in my head. My body seemed to relax. Shoulders lifted up and back, in a posture that I recognized as my own. Even my gaze softened. Somehow in that moment, by the grace of something much larger than myself, things were as they should be. Life was okay.

By then I'd lost so much that I'd reached a breaking point where I no longer had the capacity to focus on things that I couldn't actually impact.

Around that same time, in the midst of my grief, a lifelong friend abruptly stopped speaking to me. I cried once and then simply accepted it. With no warning, the dashboard in our car inexplicably lit up like a Christmas tree—without question, I took the car to the mechanic and paid whatever it cost to fix it. A stranger disagreed with something I'd said; even as a highly empathic conversationalist, I granted myself full permission to ignore them and simply not respond.

Maybe I was just too tired to give a shit. Or perhaps

my soul was overworked, and my brain was too over-crowded to focus on what I could not change.

But whatever the reason, I metamorphosed. I no longer felt the need to explain myself. I could no longer expend energy being concerned by what I could not control, including the opinions of others and the weather outside.

In the years prior to this, my mother was my why: taking care of her, making good choices, and making her proud was what I valued most. In hindsight, I spent a lifetime trying to become someone in homage to my mother so that she knew that everything she gave up and every choice she made had purpose. I'd spent my life continually striving to do better, learn more, and become the most interested and interesting version of me.

And in that moment on a frigid mid-December day, with both sadness and deep gratitude, I knew with certainty that I was free. I was finally enough. I'd exhausted the need to prove anything to anyone anymore.

That liberation is a microjoy that I could only

recognize by walking *into and through* the (figurative) fire to discover who I was to become on the other side.

## CONSIDER THIS

*In my experience, loss and grief do not get easier. In fact, the suggestion that they should is a harmful and unkind cliché. But. Loss does become more bearable. And, eventually, we transform into exactly who we need to be when we make it to the other side of whatever is yet to come.*

*At which points in your own life did you metamorphose from who you once were to who you needed to be from that moment forward? What trials have you been through that taught you the most profound lessons and perhaps, ultimately, gifted you the greatest freedom? What microjoys were hidden in the depth of what could easily be perceived as darkness? There is no rush to answer these questions, so please take all the time you need.*

# THE DAILY

Throughout my adult life, I would communicate with my mother multiple times a day, every day. Very few of my friends spoke to family as often as I did, but it was all I'd ever known. I was raised inside of a small immediate family with very little extended family to speak of. We'd been through a lot together and Mama always taught us that family came before everything. And so it did, and mostly, I didn't mind. Occasionally, though, I minded.

In the moments that I got most annoyed by my mother's somewhat random (often alarmist) texts throughout the day, I'd remind her that very few adults spoke to their parents as much as I spoke to her. "Well," she'd say in response, "they aren't my kids, Cyn. And if they were, I'd call them this often, too." Touché, Mom. Touché.

Sometimes I'd get so indignant from her calls asking for random information like "Cyn, do you remember where I put my back scratcher? I PLACED IT SOMEWHERE WEEKS AGO WHILE YOU WERE HERE VISITING?" Yes, my mother would call me at work or text me in the middle of dinner with friends to ask these kinds of questions. And damn if she wasn't right; I did remember exactly where she put the back scratcher. Again. Touché, Mom. Touché.

When she wasn't generally checking in, she'd text my husband and me the weather report along with instructions on how to best dress for the climate. It was the exact same weather report that we could access on our own phones, except her source was the local News 12, located thirty miles away. My husband and I were both in our forties and my mom would text us the local weather. Almost daily. #BringAnUmbrella.

It's been ten months since Mom died.

And every day since, I've missed her sage advice, (in)accurate weather reports, feisty opinions, and keen ability to serve up sarcasm with sentiment. All in a three-line text message.

I hope that wherever Mom is, she'll misplace things and find ways to tell me that she needs my help in finding them, once again.

A day does not pass that I don't miss her deeply. Time often drags on but sometimes, it flies by so quickly that it feels like there hasn't been a moment to grieve.

And then I wonder: remembering her, sharing stories, and laughing out loud at Mama's mothering— maybe all of this is grieving. This remembering is both deep grief and outsized joy, tangled and twisted.

Because what is remembered lives on. She is eternal through my memories.

Perhaps my grief is softened just a tiny bit for just a tiny moment by the memory of her nurturing, humor, and mamabear love.

## CONSIDER THIS

*Which relationships do you presuppose will always be available to you? How might your perspective shift if you thought about them differently? Could you momentarily find lightness, gentleness, or even humor in situations or relationships that may otherwise frustrate, annoy, or anger you?\* Is it possible to find benevolence or affection hidden between the lines or underneath what you've outwardly accepted as truth?*

\* Note: There are some relationships that simply cannot be fixed or adjusted to be anything other than what they are. Attempting to shift your response or dynamic within those experiences or relationships may cause more harm than good, so please proceed with care and discernment. In the above instance, I am not referring to harmful experiences or relationships but instead, loving and healthy ones.

# FRIENDSHIP ON
# MY DOORSTEP

Ira and I moved into a new home in a new town in the midst of the darkest times. Our new apartment was bright with sunlight and (in a scene straight out of *Snow White*) the birds chirped while the squirrels chased one another outside our front window. We painted our walls in shades of sunset yellow and coral, then hung oversized artwork throughout. We spent most of our time inside, safe in quietude. It was a strangely magical time.

As difficult as it was to move away from friends (and our previous Best Life Ever), we didn't miss the cars speeding by on the Brooklyn-Queens Expressway, the daily trudge to the grocery store, the blare of taxi horns, or the fast-paced energy that had been the brilliant background of our adult lives.

We didn't know anyone in the neighborhood yet, but on a quiet Monday morning, while I sat in our window seat, our newly installed doorbell chimed.

A friend had sent us a special delivery of the most beautiful flowers I'd ever seen. A giant bouquet filled with boldly colored full summer blooms so bright that it felt like they were grown expressly to live alongside the wild colors of our new home. Deep orange and yellow poppies; large purple, ruffled-edge parrot tulips; cream-speckled foxglove; and grapefruit-sized coral and magenta peonies. Magic.

I was so struck by the perfection of the flowers that, as the floral designer introduced herself and welcomed us to the neighborhood, I blurted out, "Since we just moved here, and you bring magic, let's be friends." (Yes, I actually said this. No, I am not ashamed. *At all.*)

It turned out that she lived a few blocks away. And we did indeed become fast friends.

Throughout the seasons of the following year, we would get coffee together and go for long walks. We'd have serious discussions but also banter about the most ridiculous things. Coincidentally, she'd once lived in Brooklyn, and we shared mutual friends. Another (unfortunate) coincidence was that her father had passed away within months of my mother's death. During a frigid winter walk, she was one of the first people I told about my breast cancer diagnosis. And months later, while sweltering under an umbrella for an outdoor summer lunch, I shared the exciting news about the imminent publishing of my next book (the one you're now holding in your hands). As the seasons continued to change, while on her way to run errands, she'd leave surprises at my door. I'd find paper bags with tomatoes from her garden or flowers saved from a previous event. I was the talker, while she was the doer, leaving tiny acts of friendship on my doorstep.

Somehow during the darkest of times, in the middle of a global pandemic, during a period of incredible loss, friendship miraculously appeared on my doorstep.

**CONSIDER THIS**

*Making new friends as adults can feel daunting and awkward. Lean into it anyway. Stay wide open to community, new friendships, and the possibility of all things. And, of course, always ask for what you want (especially when a new friend is involved).*

# EVOLVING

Lately, I've had to remind myself of who I am. I've been searching for tangible evidence of who I was before living through the hardest things. I burrow deeply into my seeking. And I remember that we are always evolving, so who I am today would have been different from who I was *then* anyway.

There are times in life when our world, unbeknownst to us, reveals a different path forward. These are moments when our lives, for whatever reason, turn inside out and upside down. Topsy-turvy and completely out of our hands.

In the span of less than one year: a global pandemic shut down the world, my nephew was killed, my mother died, my husband and I moved out of New York City where we'd lived most of our adult lives. A sibling abruptly went into heart failure and languished in the ICU for months and I was diagnosed with breast cancer. I could no longer recognize myself in the mirror. How I once existed before living through the hardest things felt obsolete. That version of myself felt like a lifetime ago. I was not *her* anymore. Or was I?

Today, I am changed. I am motherless. (Or am I? I do have a mother.) I am less my oldest nephew (in this lifetime). We no longer live in NYC. But I still exist. I'm still here. Not quite yet rooted but I am still here.

Evolving is a very strange thing. Simultaneously, we are pushed, pulled, and dragged in so many directions that it pulls us apart at the seams. And as awful as it feels in that moment, sometimes coming undone really is the *only* way. The only way to pick up what remains and shift ourselves forward. Forward to mend our brokenness and build something more beautiful. Once again.

The ground beneath me has shifted beyond my own comprehension. But in glimpses, I remember who I was. And so, I lean in. I sit. I feel. I talk. I bawl. I walk. I keep walking.

And I wait.

Until the past and present *me* finds a bridge. Until I'm firmly rooted once again.

Until the next time that I'm not. And the process starts anew.

Knowing, trusting, and believing that even when deeply changed, I will always be okay;* this faith I have may be the simplest yet most profound of *all* microjoys.

........................................................

* In this instance, "okay" doesn't mean consistently happy, consistently joyful, or unafraid. "Okay" simply means that we will make it through to the other side of whatever we are in the midst of in this lifetime. Or the next.

## CONSIDER THIS

*What do you know to be true in good times and bad? What evidence do you have that led you to this inner knowledge? Hold on to that. (If it's helpful, write it down and keep it close.) Whenever you need a beacon to help guide you to the other side of whatever you are moving through, come back to these truths. Hold tight to them and they will guide you forward forever.*

# OH, IRA

I met my husband on the Internet.

Actually, I was *introduced* to my husband on the Internet, but we met for the first time at a cafe in the Fort Greene neighborhood of Brooklyn. When I was dating, I had a rule that first dates should be held during the daytime and should not include alcohol. (I didn't want to be interested in someone over a glass of wine that I wouldn't also be intrigued by if I were fully sober during daylight.)

But back to Ira, the gorgeous man I married a few years later. I arrived on time for our Saturday 5:00 p.m.

meet and greet. (In my opinion, Internet dating isn't really dating until you meet in person and consciously choose for it to be a date. Until then, it's a meet and greet.)

Ira arrived early.

As I walked in, I recognized him right away: he wore a thick, broken-in leather jacket, well-fitted jeans, and great shoes. This man had taste and style. He waited for me to arrive before ordering tea for the both of us.

After sitting down with our mugs of piping hot tea, I noticed that he had a Target bag sitting on the counter next to him. (Why?!) I needed to understand what was *so important* that he shopped before our meeting, so I asked. And in his most confident tone, he said that he'd arrived to the neighborhood early and, since we were meeting near Target, he simply stopped by before-hand to pick up replacement filters for his water pitcher. (In my recollection, he also bought toilet paper but he insists that I added that false narrative for impact; he is correct.) But still. My eventual husband stopped en route to meeting me for the first time and ran errands.

Ira is practical and efficient.

After an hour of me staring into his soul and relentlessly asking questions, we left. Thinking we might grab a glass of wine nearby and continue talking, I asked what he was doing afterward. "I'm headed home, I'm pretty tired." Oh.

Ira is very happy to spend time in quietude.

The next day, I received a long text from him (the kind of lengthy text that should really be an email) asking, among other things, if I'd like to join him for a visit to the Metropolitan Museum of Art that afternoon. It being a Sunday, I was headed to New Jersey to visit my mom, so I wasn't available.

Ira is creative and into the arts.

We actually did meet up several more times in the coming weeks. He met me at Parsons after I finished teaching my class one night; we went out for tacos and nachos and enjoyed a glass of wine by the fireplace in the iconic Union Square Cafe (sadly, it closed a few years later). At around 1:00 a.m., we took the subway home, where he got off at my stop and walked me to my door. He didn't attempt a kiss or a handshake. Nothin'.

Ira is . . . weird.

We also met up another time at the Brooklyn Historical Society to watch a panel discussing a long-form *New York Times* story on houselessness in the city. Afterward, I had a holiday event to attend in Sunset Park, so I asked if he'd like to join me. "I think I'm going to head home, I'm pretty emotionally exhausted after that discussion." Okey dokey.

Ira is not into me. At all.

At this point, we were at least four meetings in and I had no idea if we were dating or if he just wanted to be my new best friend.

On a Friday night, after I was done volunteering (I used to volunteer doing visual merchandising for a Housing Works thrift store), I asked if he'd like to come by my apartment. I was tired and unwilling to be out anymore that evening but I did want to see him. And I'd felt comfortable and safe with him coming to my home (which was in a secure, doorman building where friends lived in surrounding units). He quickly replied that he'd be there within the hour.

I learned much later that he had had dinner at a friend's house one neighborhood away and was washing the dishes when my text came in. He dropped the dish he was holding in the sink filled with soapy water and said, "Sorry guys, I've gotta go!"

Ira does enjoy my company.

While chatting on my sofa an hour later, he interrupted what I was saying to announce, "I have a massive crush on you and I need to tell you." I invited him in for a kiss.

Ira has a massive crush on me.

Three years later, in the company of our friends and family, we married in the backyard of his childhood home, amongst the trees that were planted when he was a baby. I've never known a love so beautiful, honest, grounding, and comfortable as I do with Ira. Thank goodness for patience and time.

Oh. And also, Ira loves me.

**CONSIDER THIS**

*Patience, dear friends. Patience.*

# BREAKDOWNS, DONUTS, AND A WINTER MORNING RUN

I t had been a year since I'd walked out on my career. I was thirty-six, living in one of the most
expensive cities in the world, and I had no concrete plans for what to do with the rest of my life. At
that point, I was mostly living off my remaining sav-
ings and slowly dipping into my 401K. (Side note: This
was not a great idea and I don't recommend it.) I also
taught a small weekly meditation class in my apartment
to stay connected to the outside world while earning a
bit of money. Not enough to cover any bills but it was
*something* and I needed to be doing *something*.

It was the dead of winter and, once a week, four to six women would come over for class. They'd pile into my hallway and peel off layers of coats, boots, and bags before finding a space in my living room to place their mats. After class was over, they'd all sit around while I made a piping hot pot of chai. In hindsight, it was an incredibly special time—difficult and uncertain but also magical. I was *me* before I became the *me* that I am today. I was me . . . in the making.

Around that same time, a friend and I took up running around our neighborhood several mornings a week. I am *not* a runner. But running gave me a small sense of much-needed purpose. On one particularly cold morning, I was feeling very uncertain and highly emotional. We'd gotten as far as the local park a few blocks from my apartment before I started to bawl uncontrollably. This was not the subtle, quiet crying that some folks practice in public in New York, the kind where others notice but politely look away to give you privacy with your tears.

(It's a *thing*, ask any New Yorker.) My full-body sobbing was so obnoxious that I had to stop and sit down on a bench to catch my breath. (Side note: On a cold winter morning while wearing spandex leggings, the last thing you should do is sit down on a frigid bench.) With tears running down my face, I looked at my friend and sobbed "What the hell did I just do?! Why did I give up the life that I worked so hard to build? Nothing I do is ever going to really matter. Who do I even think I am?!"

My friend is British and this sort of public breakdown was clearly very uncomfortable for her so she took a minute before replying. (I mean, if I weren't the one in a wet heap of tears, I may have been embarrassed, too.) Embarrassed or not, friends love us anyway. And she did love me. I knew this innately when the next words that came out of her mouth were this: "Ah, come on. Your superpower is being disarming and creating connection in a way few people can. It's who you are, Cyn. Everything will work out because you are . . . you. Now. Let's go run to the donut shop, shall we? That should make this whole thing better!"*

In a city where a bottle of water is five dollars, together we had exactly three dollars in emergency money stuffed into our tiny Spandex pockets.

Like the preordained serendipity that it was, one fresh donut was exactly two-fifty.

A quick run for a warm donut topped with hibiscus icing, filled with a passion-fruit center, really did make everything better.

**CONSIDER THIS**

*Listen to your friends. In the moments that we are most confused, friends often know the exact right thing you need to soothe your temporarily broken spirit.*

. . . . . . . . . . . . . . . . . . . . . . . . . . . . . . . . . . . . . . . . . . . . .

* Good friends are often our memory keepers. While writing this essay, I had to ask my girlfriend if she recalled in more detail how this conversation went down. She did.

# JAKE

I was not a cat person. In fact, I was not a pet person at all. I was twenty-seven years old and commuting back and forth to New York City for work every day while also traveling the world in my free time. I was a "mind my own business because I'm too busy" kind of woman. So, in an extraordinary act of poetic justice, a very cute kitten in a very large box showed up in my line of vision.

Each Saturday morning, I'd go to the local bagel shop for a toasted everything bagel with cream cheese, cut in four pieces. It was a simple routine:

Wait in line.

Order my bagel.

Add half-and-half to a cup of subpar deli coffee.

Pick up my bagel.

Go home.

This was the way it always was.

Until one Saturday morning, when the shop owner proudly unveiled something in a box out front. A small crowd gathered.

Bagel in hand, I walked out to see what was happening: inside the box were seven of the cutest kittens I'd ever laid eyes on. And in something akin to a feeding frenzy, people started grabbing them. And . . . taking them! To where? For what? Were all these people looking for kittens before this moment? Or did this box just appear and then they decided they wanted one? *What the hell was happening?*

Within seconds, only one short-haired and one long-haired, blue-eyed kitten remained.

Around the same time, a little girl exclaimed to her mom that they *had* to get a kitten. Her mom, ever practical, accepted the challenge but said that they would have to take two because "kittens are best in pairs."

My brain spiraled quickly from a "mind my own business because I'm too busy" mode of existence into that of an eccentric cat lady. The words that flashed across my mind were "I know they're going to take the long-haired kitten; I know it! . . . I MUST TAKE THIS CAT NOW BEFORE THE CHILD DOES!"

Without thinking, I scooped up the long-haired kitten and yelled, "Thanks, Sharon!" (the kitten purveyor/bagel shop owner) and ran to my car without looking back. I could feel the steely-eyed judgment from the remaining people behind me, including the child and her mother. I moved even faster toward my car: a judgment-free oasis.

*Why did I grab that cat?!*

In a (not at all) surprising turn of events, I spent the

entire afternoon trying to give away the kitten. I called every responsible adult I could think of and no one, including my own mother, would take him. To sweeten the deal, I went to the pet store and purchased all kinds of fancy cat paraphernalia. Still, no takers.

I was now officially ~~the owner of~~ owned by a temperamental long-haired, blue-eyed cat. One who is sitting across from me as I type these words. He now has green eyes.

It's been fifteen years since that Saturday and Jake, my most loyal and affectionate comrade, still requires all kinds of fancy cat paraphernalia.

And as with so many microjoys, some seemingly clairvoyant being knew something that I didn't: there is no such thing as being ready. For pets. For partners. For children. For opportunities. For challenges. For sorrow. For grief. For love.

There is no such thing as being ready, but when we must, we will become so.

As was the case when someone or something beyond me had the foresight to know that Jake and I would spend a lifetime happily antagonizing one another.

**CONSIDER THIS**

*The world is too fickle for readiness. Instead of striving or waiting for readiness, consider this: when that kitten, person, or opportunity shows up in your line of vision, you are already ready enough to accept whatever microjoys await.*

# FRIENDSHIP JUST IN TIME

I used to have rigid ideals about how friends should show up, how they should respond, and what they should do in times of need and times of plenty. But the last few difficult years have shifted those beliefs dramatically. The reality of being an adult, a flawed human, an imperfect being, is that we hold contradicting truths and multiple identities simultaneously. A friend who is a parent might be struggling to remember who they are in this brand-new world. The friend who just started a demanding new job is navigating adulthood as the grown-up *new kid* again. That other friend going through a rough patch is reassessing everything she once believed to be true about her life. Navigating multiple experiences can be exciting but it's also complicated and exhausting. At any time, given so many roles and identities, we are often trying to find our footing. Over and over again.

When it relates to friendships, a light touch, patience, and a whole lot of loving forgiveness are vital, but sometimes in short supply.

Below is a note that I received from a dear friend many months after going through the hardest things. I hadn't heard much from her throughout the ordeal but I hadn't reached out, either. Her unexpected note stirred a reawakening for me, a coming home again to the world outside, a much-needed reminder that it would soon be time to reemerge. I felt like a rattled snow globe, mostly calm but also shaken and unsettled.

*hi cyndie,*

*i miss you and think of you often, every other day maybe, your smile and wild hair, bright lipstick and big laugh. i'm so proud of who you are: how loyal you are to yourself, how your voice comes through in your writing and photos, how dedicated you are to your loved ones and strangers alike.*

    *i'd love to catch up soon. so much has changed for both of us since we last saw each other, but this email, right now, is simply to say that i love you and i think about how beautiful you are more than you'll ever believe. i am confident that the same goes for so many others. how about that, huh? i thought you should know.*

*your friend*

*– m*

As with many friendships that ebb and flow with time, I didn't know that I needed to hear from her exactly in that moment, but I did. Our friends may not be available in all ways, always, but that doesn't make their friendship any less meaningful. They often show up as they can, exactly as we need them, even when we are unaware that we do.

Genuine friendships—even as they evolve with time—are an undeniable gift in this lifetime. And when we struggle with our own expectations of others, it helps to acknowledge that, just like us, our friends are doing the best they can with what they have, in any particular moment.

**CONSIDER THIS**

*Friends become our mirrors and show us who we truly are; they are also our memory keepers as life flows and we forget the moments that made us. When we are lucky enough to have them, friendships that shift and grow with time are soul-fueling. So whenever possible, show kindness, assume love, and forgive most things.*

# SO MANY FEELINGS

I used to wonder if I felt *too* much—if I experienced moments of joy and beauty too fully while savoring the details of every tiny, gorgeous thing that brought me happiness, from brightly hued flowers and neon-colored Birkenstocks to conversations shared with strangers and chirping birds outside the window. I sometimes noticed that my outward expression of enthusiasm in witnessing small, beautiful things became (almost) contagious. People around me would also become excited, passionate, and expressive. They'd boldly make their own declarations and, when they did, they appeared happier and lighter than they were before.

I also wondered if I felt moments of anger too deeply when it sent me reeling with indignation and righteousness about inequity, dishonesty, and all manner of shitty behaviors. But speaking out and *not* sitting idly by also became contagious; people who were once indifferent, who preferred to "mind their own business," became more engaged, beginning to understand that inequity is *everyone's* business. They, too, started to create small changes within their homes, workplaces, and local communities, reading new kinds of books, watching more inclusive movies, and having difficult but necessary conversations.

I still secretly wondered why other people didn't find the need to express things as deeply as I did. What was wrong with me?

With time, I've come to appreciate the way I experience the fullness of my emotions—without the guardrails of feigned politeness that limit most people. I've learned that expressiveness is permission-granting for those around us to feel whatever they feel.

Emotions and feelings can be fleeting, and sometimes fade as quickly as they arise. But there are also occasions where they don't (anger about inequity, for example). I've learned that this, too, is okay. The more we allow our thoughts and emotions to come to the surface, the more likely it is that we'll work through them and get to the other side.

### CONSIDER THIS

*In a world that asks us to be quiet—to push down our feelings—to make others more comfortable, there is bravery in acknowledging the fullness of what we feel. Though you may not know it at this particular moment, it is my experience that our honest acknowledgment is permission-granting and confidence-building to the people around us.*

# LEONARD

I moved into the only apartment building on a tiny block in Brooklyn. It was a former piano factory, and the instant I caught a glimpse of the high ceilings and light-flooded living room, I was in love. Aside from the apartment building, there wasn't much else to see on that block. On one side was a large, dilapidated storage space and on the other, a seventy-five-year-old uniform shop that carried uniforms for everyone from the NYPD to students. I lived in that apartment for five years and during that time, I witnessed the evolution of an entire neighborhood.

People came and went, buildings were repurposed, and a coffee shop was built where an empty lot once stood. But still, the fig tree in the community garden kept growing, the summer festivals continued. And year after year, Leonard meandered the neighborhood and traversed the block that my building was on.

Shortly after I moved in, the storage facility next door sold. For months following, I watched people move lifetimes' worth of memories out of that building. Some moved them into double-parked vans while others simply left their memories at the curb for garbage pickup. That's when I started to notice Leonard. He was probably in his late sixties at the time, a tall, thin, unassuming man with short gray hair and slightly bent posture. He always seemed to be wearing something in a shade of brown while quietly pacing the street. After seeing him a few times, I stopped to introduce myself. "I'm Cyndie, I live in that building over there and I always see you around, so I thought I'd say hi." "I'm

Leonard," he said. "Nice to meet ya." And so began a yearslong fellowship with Leonard.

Here's what I came to know.

Leonard had been in the military. For years after he came back, he'd lived throughout Brooklyn, most recently in a rooming house in a building a few neighborhoods away. When the building was torn down, without a new place to live, all his belongings were moved into the storage unit next door to my apartment building. After moving in and out of shelters for a few months, he finally settled on the idea of simply staying where his belongings were. And so, he moved himself into the storage unit, too. (This was not legal, but it was a self-service facility and there were no employees that I'd ever seen.) When the storage facility was sold, Leonard and his belongings, again, had to find another way. It was summertime, so from what I could gather, he'd sleep in parks or shelters, then wash up in the bathrooms at the hospital nearby and hang out in the neighborhood minding his own business, cup of coffee in hand. I never found out where his belongings went, though.

Leonard was always incredibly kind, and we were happy to run into each other. "Hey, Leonard, I'm grabbing a coffee, want one?" He'd look up and a big smile would come over his face. "How you doin' today?" Every now and again when I'd see him, he'd forget who I was and we'd go through the introductions all over again. Mostly, though, we'd banter like we'd been friends forever. (Though we could hold a ten-minute conversation, I don't think he remembered much from day to day.) After my (soon to be) husband started hanging out at my place, I introduced him to Leonard, too.

On one occasion, I must've looked flustered and especially stressed rushing under the scaffolding toward the subway because after I shouted, "Hey, Leonard! You better stop smoking, it's not good for you," he smiled his big smile and said, "I know, I know. Hey, you doin' alright? You're moving awfully fast, you need some money?" He then pulled out a twenty-dollar bill and told me to take it. That was Leonard. He may not have always remembered my name, but he knew when he saw someone who could use some help. I didn't take the twenty-dollar bill, but he kept trying to give it to me anyway.

Not long after that, I moved to a different neighborhood because my apartment, too, was sold. I did see Leonard a few more times before we left. I told him where we were moving to and that I hoped I'd see him again. He smiled that big smile and said, "Oh yeah, that neighborhood is real nice. I'm over there sometimes. I'll see you."

Two years later, my husband and I were walking down Fulton Street and there, sitting on a bench in an army green sweater with matching oversized sweatpants, was . . . Leonard! I was so happy to see him and as soon as I yelled out his name, he looked up with that big smile and said, "Heeeeyy! It's you. How y'all doing?

And how's Brooklyn Heights treatin' you?" Leonard knew exactly who we were and remembered what we'd spoken about years before. Leonard was Leonard. We chatted for fifteen minutes, and he repeated some of what we already knew but also, he let us know that he was doing alright.

In all the time I knew him, I never did see Leonard in conversation with anyone else, but seeing him in the neighborhood, day in and day out, was a consistent source of familiarity and joy for me. I hope it was mutual.

In big cities and small towns, as we rush around seeking our next big adventure, we easily take for granted the people who surround us. We often see folks and never stop to say hello, banter, or even consider that they, too, have a story to share. They do. We all do. And though he may not realize it, being in fellowship with Leonard was an incredible microjoy during my lifetime.

## CONSIDER THIS

*Who are the people that you see often but have never actually spoken to? Could you introduce yourself or start a conversation? You could begin by sharing some of your story with them. Consider how exchanging stories of our lived experiences might shift, or even entirely transform, the lens through which we see the world.*

## JUST WALKING

Right now, I'm walking.

Underneath a colorful facade of fabulous head wraps and high-waisted jeans, I have a wild internal life filled with deep thoughts, big dreams, and way too many patterns. I am an active overthinker and I spend a lot of time alone, particularly since moving out of New York City.

I sometimes miss my formerly overscheduled life. I sometimes miss running to this plane or that lunch or the thing happening uptown. I sometimes miss casually meeting a friend for a glass of wine on a random

Tuesday night that ends with us quietly closing down our favorite little neighborhood spot. I miss the kinds of places where the crew would check in quietly but also allow us to slowly savor a beautiful glass (or two) of wine for hours at the end of a quiet evening.

Sometimes I miss that life. But not often. Because I'm tired.

I'd worked two jobs from the age of sixteen and continued to work multiple jobs throughout college. I started my career at twenty-one, began traveling the world and climbing up the corporate ladder while failing miserably in my personal life. Then I was thirty-five and starting a new career, then thirty-seven and finding my voice again. And when I was nearly forty, I was getting married. Then at forty-one, considering children but not necessarily wanting to be pregnant (because it sounds awful and painful and I'm too old to feel interested in the act of physically carrying anyone other than myself). Then I was forty-two and the world around me collapsed.

Today, I'm forty-four—still so young, but my shoulders are slumped from bearing the weight of it all. And I'm exhausted.

When I quit my former career, I went headfirst into discovering Cyndie 2.0. And she (I) emerged quickly because I was always her.

But still. I was running. I was running toward all the excitement of my long-hoped-for acceptance and community. I was also running away. I was running away from being a child of poverty in a wealthy world. I was still learning what it meant to have money when people close to me didn't. I was running away from the reality of navigating being biracial Black in my very white world. I was running away from the impact of being a part of vastly different worlds but still feeling a deep sense of belonging and loyalty to all of them.

And so for now, I'm walking. Quietly. Patiently. Until I'm ready to run again. And I will because I love running. But right now, I'm called to be quiet and just walk.

## CONSIDER THIS

*You may not need to walk right now. And even if you do, your version of walking and mine may be very different. If you feel compelled to slow down and go inward for a time, in whatever way makes sense for your situation, do that. But maybe you've been walking long enough and you're ready to slowly jog, or hell, even run. If that is true for you, then take steps to pick up your own pace. Either way, be mindful of when and how you may be "keeping up with Joneses" and forgetting to keep pace with yourself.*

# TOO EARLY FOR
# SOFT PANTS

After a recent snowstorm, my husband and I spent much of the weekend inside wearing soft pants with thick sweaters. Though it wasn't actually cold inside, there is something about wearing a warm sweater or wool housecoat that makes me *feel* much cozier. I go into a full sloth mood during the winter, with no concern for getting properly dressed or venturing outdoors, except to the porch to collect packages filled with unnecessary things.

Ira, on the other hand, is from hearty Minnesota stock. He must go outside every single day to walk for a few miles, regardless of the inclement weather. He doesn't believe in wearing anything other than jeans or well-fitting pants outdoors, or in front of other people that aren't me—so no soft pants for him unless it's after 10:00 p.m. and we are alone in our home. He is very serious about this rule and won't even take the garbage out while wearing his (very stylish, spattered-indigo-dyed) sweatpants because he insists that they are for *indoor use only*. I am confused by this because when we moved to the suburbs during the pandemic, I gave up all semblance of "hard" clothing including my footwear, which now consists of many, many variations of Birkenstocks (shearling versions worn with socks in the winter and patent leather versions worn without socks in the summer).

As I sat in the living room, likely pondering world peace or watching reruns of *The Golden Girls*, I realized that I hadn't seen Ira in a while. In this case, "a while" meant thirty minutes or so. We live in a two-bedroom apartment so it is not easy to be out of sight of one another. There is literally nowhere to go. Alarmed, I removed my extra-thick fleece blanket from my lap and got up to look for him.

I found him in our warmly lit bedroom sitting half up, knees bent, dressed in a well-worn pink T-shirt, soft pants, and wool socks (this casual attire typically doesn't happen at this early-ish hour). Jake was leisurely lying on one side of him and a favorite oversized mug filled with (probably) bourbon was on the other. Alongside the mug was a partially read book that was now functioning only to prop up his phone—I'm not sure why. In his lap was an iPad that glowed yellow from the screen light.

Seeing him, that moment, felt like home. Headphones in, invested in his (probably terrible\*) movie, he didn't notice me peek in on him. So I went back to the living room to grab my phone and snap a picture. Just because.

........................................................

\* Though highly discerning in so many ways, Ira has very bad taste in movies. Not always but . . . often. He knows it, admits it, and is quite pleased with himself about it anyway.

## CONSIDER THIS

*Over the past decade, I've taken to capturing everyday occurrences with my phone camera or through journaling. Each moment represents a tiny bit of life that has passed, moments that won't occur again in the exact same way. And I peruse these pictures and reread my own entries when I need a reminder that life, in all of its imperfections, is still so remarkably beautiful.*

*Are there ways that you might enjoy capturing everyday moments? You could paint, journal, share stories, write, take pictures, text friends, record audio—the options are infinite. Find what feels right for you.*

# PAPA WAS A
# ROLLING STONE

My father always had a complicated relationship with his children, but I was the youngest and, as far as parenting goes, I got the best parts of him.

He called me Sugar Bear and often told me how proud of me he was and how very special I was. He also told anyone else who would listen. Daddy was from North Carolina and being up north most of his adult life still never took the country outta this man. In fact, he always pronounced my name as "Sidney." He knew my name was "Cyndie" but it certainly never sounded like that when he pronounced it with his deep Southern drawl. I teased him mercilessly about this and he loved that I did.

Though we were different, I always admired his ability to never take life too seriously (he let my mom handle the things that needed to be taken seriously). No matter the situation though, we always found a way to stay profoundly connected. Even as a little kid, I'd forgive easily without judgment, and I think Daddy always appreciated that, even if he didn't have the language to express it.

In fact, I was the one he called when he knew he was dying. I'm certain he thought that I *wouldn't* judge him for admitting this truth out loud. I think he believed that this admission was a failure; him acknowledging that *he felt* that his death was imminent was letting us down. I did judge him though. I remember it vividly: As I was getting into my brand-new, caramel-colored Nissan Murano, my phone rang from the hospital and, with certainty, Dad said, "Sugar Bear, I'm dying." I told him that it wasn't true and that he wasn't allowed to say that to me. I was not okay with him admitting that deep and painful truth. So, he apologized.

He passed away a month later in January. I was twenty-eight years old at the time.

A friend had convinced me to attend a (somewhat cult-y) self-help forum the previous year, and as part of the process we were asked to actively forgive people in our lives. To call them, acknowledge whatever they had done, and forgive them. It wasn't quite as simple as this, but this was the gist of it. I remember calling my parents at 10:00 p.m. and asking to talk to my dad. My mom handed him the phone and I said, "I forgive you, Daddy. I know you did the best you could with what you had." He didn't know how to reply so he just said, "Okay, baby," and that was it, no questions asked.

But I know that he knew in his heart that I forgave him for having a drinking problem and being a nomad much of our lives; I forgave his imperfection at fatherhood and I loved him anyway.

My father had an eighth-grade education but could make anything out of anything. An old toilet became a pink planter for the side of our house. An accumulation of McDonald's Happy Meal toys were the perfect items for an under-the-stairs terrarium. Random pieces of found wood became a simple pool shack where we could change from wet clothes into dry ones. Old liquor of all kinds made the best damn moonshine around. (I don't know this firsthand. It looked like battery acid, but he and his friends would hang out long into the night drinking and laughing. So I think it's a fair guesstimation on my part.)

Papa was a rolling stone but also a magician. And I am forever grateful for him. In spite of everything, because of him, I am.

## CONSIDER THIS

*Relationships can be complicated. Navigating the depth of our full feelings is challenging, particularly with our parents. But it is possible. As we grow and find our place in this great big world, we learn perspective. Should we have the capacity to make the choice, we might access resources, like therapy, to do our own necessary inner work, to let go of what doesn't serve our growth, and to learn to accept what we cannot change.*

*I will not suggest that I understand the full complexity of relationships, particularly ones that are not my own. But I do know that in my life, letting go of the things I am unable to change about the people I love has given me an incredible gift of freedom.*

*I had a semi-present father who rode an old beat-up bicycle around town (instead of a car) and had other children interwoven between us along the way. And, still, he was one of my great loves. He taught me that there is always a purpose for everything and everyone. He taught me to hold on gently and always laugh while I did. He wasn't a serious man and, in part because of him, I've found the ability to find humor and microjoys in all things.*

*When my family gathers, we have the biggest belly laughs and the best damn stories about my dad and his ability to create something out of nothing. And what a gift that is despite everything else.*

# THE WEIRD LAWN
# CHAIR PEOPLE

Ira and I really like vintage lawn chairs—the collapsible loungers with brightly colored nylon webbing and a nearly unbreakable (though not very sturdy) aluminum frame. Be warned: that frame will singe off the top layer of your skin if you don't cover the metal arms when lounging in the hot sun. But danger be damned, the nostalgia is worth a minor burn from time to time. There is an innately calming quality about these lounge chairs. Looking at them makes me want to slow down and rest with a good book while drinking iced lemonade (sometimes, but not always, spiked with bourbon).

When we moved to the suburbs, we scouted for months to find vintage lawn chairs in mint condition that didn't cost a small fortune. We eventually found a rare perfect pair; one has taupe-and-white-colored webbing and the other is kelly green and white. Though they weren't the bright colors we were initially looking for, they are pure perfection. We picked them up in a nearby small town from an older gentleman who told us that the chairs once belonged to his parents and he'd found them while cleaning out the garage. We chatted for a moment and piled the chairs into our car to head off into the sunset with our newly acquired pieces of Americana.

In the midst of all this scouting, we forgot a few simple things: we don't actually own a lawn to place these chairs lovingly onto, nor do we own a home that we can sit in front of while waving to the neighbors when we look up from our fantastic books. Of course, we could take them to the park and the beach, but the front lawn experience is why we wanted the lawn chairs.

After much consideration, we decided that we would

be okay being known as the Weird Lawn Chair People in Front of the Apartment Building in our neighborhood. If it came down to that, I mean.

So on a summer Sunday afternoon, I donned my oversized yellow straw hat and we pulled our chairs— along with our newspaper, a few good books, and two cans of very cold beverages—onto the small patch of lawn in front of our building. (The hat was multipurpose; it blocked the sun but also functioned as a disguise in case this was too weird and someone recognized me.) In New York City, where land is in short supply but high demand, sitting on your stoop in front of your apartment building is normal and even enviable. But here in our suburban neighborhood, it was slightly out of place alongside the million-dollar homes lining our street. Still, we persisted. And throughout the day while lounging, we watched drivers glance over in curiosity, chatted with people (who we presumed to be neighbors) out with their dogs, and eventually pulled out a third chair for another neighbor while we opened up a bottle of wine and chatted into the evening.

Our vintage lawn chairs brought us community, comfort, and nostalgia.

Long live the Weird Lawn Chair People. May we know them. May we raise them. May we *be* them.

**CONSIDER THIS**

*With perspective, embarrassing ourselves on lawn furniture is a good dilemma to have—so buy the lawn chairs. And use them. Should you choose to be in a relationship, consider finding a partner who is thrilled to be a lawn chair oddball right alongside you. Don't allow the possible opinions of others to diminish your own sense of curiosity, lightheartedness, and fun. Always choose tiny thrills, big joys, and vintage lawn furniture, whether you have a lawn or not.*

# FREUDENFREUDE (JOY FOR OTHERS' JOY)

There's a German word that I learned years ago while watching the Broadway play *Avenue Q*: schadenfreude. It loosely translates to mean pleasure derived from another person's misfortune, failure, or trouble. Most of us, when we're being most honest, have experienced this feeling. Consider the tiny but smug smile that forms on the corners of our mouths when hearing that a particularly awful person didn't get their way (it was their comeuppance, wasn't it?), or the satisfying "fail" videos that we watch on television (what were they even thinking?), or the mortifying

"Oh, thank God it's not me" when someone *else* is having a rough time. Feelings of schadenfreude may not occur during our proudest moments, but it is a human feeling nonetheless.

And. But.

Because humanity is both ironic and wonderful, I recently learned another German word from a woman in my community: freudenfreude, which loosely translates as the joy we feel at the success and joy of others.

Isn't that beautiful?

Learning this word brought me such delight. Though I've certainly felt schadenfreude, I more often feel massive amounts of joy when bearing witness to other people's joy. I am thrilled by seeing other people happy. Overjoyed, even. Consider when a dear friend enthusiastically shares their big, exciting news, a child spots their favorite person and breaks into toothless glee, or perfect strangers get engaged in the center of Times Square. *How absolutely joyful!*

Joy, kindness, and generosity have a magical quality

of contagiousness (in a good way), which is perhaps why freudenfreude is often my default. Also (unscientifically, of course) feeling joy for others makes our skin look more glowy, our friendships more enduring, and our teeth appear whiter, too. (That last line may be a bit of a stretch but it can't hurt to manifest it, right?)

As in most things in life, there is equilibrium—though hopefully imbalanced in favor of the side of joy.

## CONSIDER THIS

*Joy feels magnified when experienced in the company of others. It seems to multiply in the most magnificent ways. When you find yourself in situations that celebrate the joy of loved ones or strangers, consciously choose to soak it in and feel their joy. Allow it to permeate inward and outward.*

*And, because life happens, when you are not able to find joy in the joy of others, that, too, is okay (and often temporary). Instead, take care of your-self without the added pressure of needing to feel disingenuously joyful. When the time comes that you can again feel joy in the joy of others, it will be that much more genuine and joyful. In the meantime, for every feeling of schadenfreude, I wish you one hundred times more feelings of freudenfreude.*

# A 3:00 A.M. STRANGER
## AT THE DOOR

Still wearing a cast after foot surgery (and also after surviving the hardest things), my brother was on his way home to New Jersey from a long-deserved vacation. But his three-hour flight was delayed by thirteen hours. The flight was initially postponed, then postponed again, then canceled, then reinstated to fly into a different airport. After fifteen hours, his flight finally landed at a very small airport two and a half hours away from his destination. It was two o'clock in the morning on his birthday. The entire scenario was so absurd. He and eighty-nine other passengers were left in a very small airport with only two employees and zero transportation options to get to their destinations. Have I mentioned that it was two o'clock in the morning? On his birthday?

With my mom gone, my brothers and I have become even closer. Given that, I was the lucky one he texted at 2:00 a.m. After being startled awake by the chime of the text, I immediately called him back. In a flurry of chaotic early-morning activity, most of the passengers were unable to get a car service. I tried on my end while my brother (plus the eighty-nine other passengers) also attempted the impossible feat. After a few minutes on the car service app, I was magically given an option for a premium car with a quicker pickup; I immediately booked it. I excitedly called my brother to let him know that I was breaking him out (it felt like a prison break!), to which he replied, "Oh, I can't take that, sis. This guy has been helping me with my luggage and everything since this morning. I can't leave him here. I'll try to get transportation to Newark airport so he can get his car." My reply: "NO. Absolutely no. It's 2:00 a.m. I was able to book you a car to our apartment; you *will* get into the car." We exchanged a few more words and I hung up. Except.

Being my empathetic mother's daughter and empathetic brother's sister, I knew he was right. So I called him back and said that the new friend should come with him and get another car from our place to Newark airport, which would be much closer and easier to access. Within minutes, he returned my call to say that the new friend wouldn't be joining him since he had a few people with him and graciously said that my brother should head home without him. Phew, no strangers after all!

Except.

My brother reached out once again to let me know he had picked up another stranded stranger to share a ride with him to our home at (now) three o'clock in the morning: an older man on the same flight. As we went over the arrangements for my brother and this stranger, he offered us money for our assistance. I couldn't accept his money, so in gratitude, he invited my husband and me to his wife's highway bar fifteen miles away for complimentary drinks. It was very kind and also a very strange offer at that very late hour.

I got back into bed and thought about how to explain this scenario (including the stranger en route to our apartment) to my husband. And out of nowhere, I burst into laughter. I could not believe how ridiculous it was: my adult brother was stranded on his birthday at an airport hours away in the middle of the night after his first vacation in years. My husband was asleep. And the very-best-case scenario included bringing an eighty-five-plus-year-old perfect stranger to our home in the middle of the night while I was half awake and in pajamas.

I was exhausted and the whole thing was so comical that I couldn't help but roll my eyes, remember the heartache of the prior two years, and say through un-controllable laughter, "What a ridiculous and fabulous inconvenience this whole scenario actually is!"

## CONSIDER THIS

*In this beautifully topsy-turvy world, perspective changes everything.*

# HOW TO LEAD

When I was in my late twenties, I was a young manager working in corporate fashion. I had a brilliant team reporting to me and a director that I deeply respected. (Actually, when I think back *without* my rose-tinted glasses, one of my direct reports disliked me with a passion so deep that I questioned my own capabilities for a very long while. But in time, as most things go, my confidence grew and the questioning eventually passed.)

Part of our responsibility in the product development team was placing orders for materials, which seems easy enough, but it's actually a tedious process that takes a lot of organization and detail. Neither of which were skills that I had at that point, nor did I think I needed them. Clearly, I did.

One day, I was called into my director's office. Hardworking and eager to please, I quickly sat down in the chair in her glass-enclosed space. She asked me to close the door behind me and I immediately felt like we were in a fishbowl.

She took off her designer glasses and gently put them down on her desk while looking me straight in the eye in a way that was kind but also direct. Apparently, there was an order error that had occurred on our team. It cost the company approximately thirty-five thousand dollars. Thirty-five thousand dollars! I didn't know what to say. I had no idea how it happened. But I knew that as the team leader, it was my responsibility nonetheless. This thirty-five-thousand-dollar loss was my fault.

My eyes teared up and then overflowed. I was certain that I was being fired. The more tears fell, the longer it seemed that she sat there in silence until she finally broke the spell by handing me a box of tissues and asking a simple question: "Are you done?"

Yes. I guess I was. And in one very long rambling sentence, a version of this spilled out of my mouth: "I'm sorry. I really don't know how this happened but it's my fault and it should not have happened. I'm sorry."

Her reply was simple. "Okay. I believe you."

Okay? *Okay?!* That was all she had to say while I sat before her, red-faced, in a heap of tears, before she fired me?

"I don't really know what that means. *What* is okay? What happens now?"

"Well. You're very talented, our team is incredible, your people skills are excellent, and you're a strong manager. Is this mistake going to happen again?"

My answer was short and to the point: "No. No it isn't."

"Very good. Then unless you have more questions, we're done here," she stated with finality.

And that was it. No badgering, micromanaging, re-assessing, or taking back her original feedback. She meant what she said and we moved forward.

I grew with the company for several more years and she eventually became vice president. At some point, while in the throes of a full-time career, I applied and got accepted into a renowned graduate school program that required that I travel for weeks at a time to Paris, Hong Kong, and New York. Not only did she burst with pride as she congratulated me, but she also signed off for our company to pay for much of my graduate school education. She taught me how to communicate openly, situationally lead, and elevate my team so that they could (and willingly would) hold down the fort while I was studying abroad. When I graduated, my thesis was one of three chosen to present to industry executives. And when I did, she was in the back row smiling proudly and watching my yearslong effort come to fruition.

It was not lost on me that she believed in me. She

understood that the company could afford the loss and knew that a long, drawn-out conversation admonishing me was neither necessary nor helpful. A mistake happened and it wouldn't happen again. She trusted me and she trusted our team. And because of that, I learned to better trust myself. And of course, that same mistake never did happen again. In fact, very few mistakes followed.

She went on to become my mentor for many years after I left that job, and to this day, we are still very good friends.

## CONSIDER THIS

*Some of the most important lessons that I learned in my career working for others were those I learned that day: Treat folks with respect and dignity and they will do everything they can to do right by you.*

*Say what you mean and mean what you say. Acknowledge mistakes and hold people accountable, but also leave room for humanity and growth. Leave space for conversation but sometimes, less is much more impactful.*

# CONCLUSION

## · THE WISDOM OF IMPERMANENCE

*Every experience that you have is simply one moment in time.*

*Every moment that you struggle within, sit with, or dance your way through will eventually pass.*

*This truth applies to all things—the good stuff and the difficult, the darkness and the light, the just and the unjust. It is all transient, momentary.*

*There is both grace and wisdom in knowing that this moment, too, will eventually pass.*

—CYNDIE SPIEGEL, *A YEAR OF POSITIVE THINKING: DAILY INSPIRATION, WISDOM, AND COURAGE*

Within these pages, we've explored the depth and breadth of what it means to recognize joy in the midst of a life lived. Joy in the middle of all things. Joy while we are rooted but also when we are deeply unmoored. It is possible to find joy alongside grief but also inside of everyday comforts. To uncover joy in the midst of turmoil but also in the depth of calm. Joy is still extraordinary, even when bittersweet.

It is our birthright to experience wild, simple, and beautiful joy while living a perfectly imperfect life. We were born for this.

We've learned that joy and grief are intimate dance partners in this lifetime. And if we want to dance, we must also be willing to grieve because we live life on a spectrum that includes many emotions and a range of feelings. Experiencing hard things is not optional; we must choose hope and joy when we are able to. Over and over again.

Microjoys teach us that life is *all* things and despite

it all, there is always joy to be discovered. Hope to be had. Laughter to heal us. Wonderment to temporarily consume our worries. Memories to make. Moments to notice. We now know that we deserve to experience the respite of joy, even on the fringes of the hardest things.

We may experience the depth of despair and sadness, but also the height of astonishing happiness. We will grieve, we may lose hope, and there could be moments when we feel that this big beautiful life of ours is simply too much to bear. It is not. We can go on, one foot in front of the other, until we recognize that we are deserving of joy once again. And when that moment appears, we will continue our pursuit of microjoys and begin to rediscover whatever beauty awaits us. Beauty *will* await us the moment we allow ourselves to bear witness to it.

Throughout the writing of this book, I've lived and relived some of the most beautiful and difficult times in my own life. Over and over again, I was reminded of the sublime power in microjoys. I've learned that joy comes from the depths of hope, perspective, experience, resilience, and awareness. It does not come from money, status, education, perfection, or anyone outside of ourselves.

We will continue to experience the topsy-turviness of being alive. But. And. It is still our God-given right to feel good, joyful, and happy, too. Each of us has the profound ability to uncover joy (almost) everywhere. And in the rare moments when we can't, we learn to trust that in due time and with patience, our faith in the possibility of joy will eventually reemerge.

Until then, we sit, we listen, we dance, we cry, we feel, we walk, we fall, we dust off, and in time, we begin to rise once again.

Because of . . . and in spite of . . . everything.

I owe a deep bow of gratitude to you, dear reader and friend. Writing this book has been both healing and hopeful. I've laughed so hard that I've snorted and cried tears so deep that they've swallowed me whole, but only momentarily until I reached the other side.

Throughout this book, I've felt so many feelings, but overwhelmingly these stories have brought me home to my own joy once again.

My audacious hope is that my words might possibly inspire the same for you; a reminder that as you are, and as life is, there is always the capacity for a lifetime filled with hope and joy, amidst all else.

And for that, I am eternally grateful.

# ACKNOWLEDGMENTS

Thank you to my agent, Wendy Sherman, for believing in the wisdom of microjoys. Thank you to the team at Penguin Life for believing in my words. And an extra special thank you to Margaux Weisman, Amy Sun, and Meg Leder for coaxing those words into a masterful book.

Thank you to my husband, Ira, for always being my safe haven. Your deep capacity to love me* is what

---

* Even when I look like hell and scold our cats for being furry little attention seekers.

allows me to move through the world with generosity and confidence. Thanks for being my matching mitten. I love you. A lot.

Thank you to my parents: In life, you both taught me to love who I am, express myself boundlessly, and find humor in all things. Oh, and you also taught me to find joy in gardening and in picking up other people's curbside trash to recycle it into something more beautiful. (Except for that one bug-infested chair that I picked up in the early 2000s that led to nothing but heartbreak and roaches. That was awful.) And still. I love you both beyond words and will miss you, always. Until we meet again.

Thank you to my brothers: Your bottomless love, ridiculous humor, and ability to take way too damn long to tell stories, even in the face of tragedy and loss, is what gave me the courage to write this book. I love you.

Thank you to my nephews: RBS, DCS, and BDS. I'm proud of you and I love you.

Thank you to Aunt Doll for loving and accepting

me fully, always. May you be resting in love with all the soul food, faith, and church music that eternity has to offer.

Thank you to Mama and Papa H. for your kindness, support, and genuine love. And also for wine by the fire and always allowing us to camp in your backyard under the big sky and bright stars of Minnesota. Oh, and thanks for letting us get married there, too.

Thank you to Geovana, Tamsin, Yolanda, Trae, Cristy T., and Tash for your eternal friendship—it means more than you know.

Thank you to Susan for being my longtime therapist, my teacher, and even, at times, my surrogate auntie.

Thank you to Amy and Shamira for always holding down the fort. Truly, I'm not sure how I'd get any work done without you.

And finally, thank you to the Dear Grown Ass Women community: When my world fell apart at the seams, you collectively helped stitch me back together while still being advocates for one another. I am eternally grateful to each of you for believing in the power of genuine community, especially Naomi, Eunice, Bree, Jennifer, Renia, and EB.

I have so many people to thank who have supported me along the way, including my extended social media community who've grown with me for many years, and my GS10K family (especially Los Jeffersons). I already know that I'll forget to write many of you into these acknowledgments, so in advance, please accept my apology—it wasn't purposeful. I love you and I am eternally grateful that you are in my life.